Kickoff Foundation
Workbook

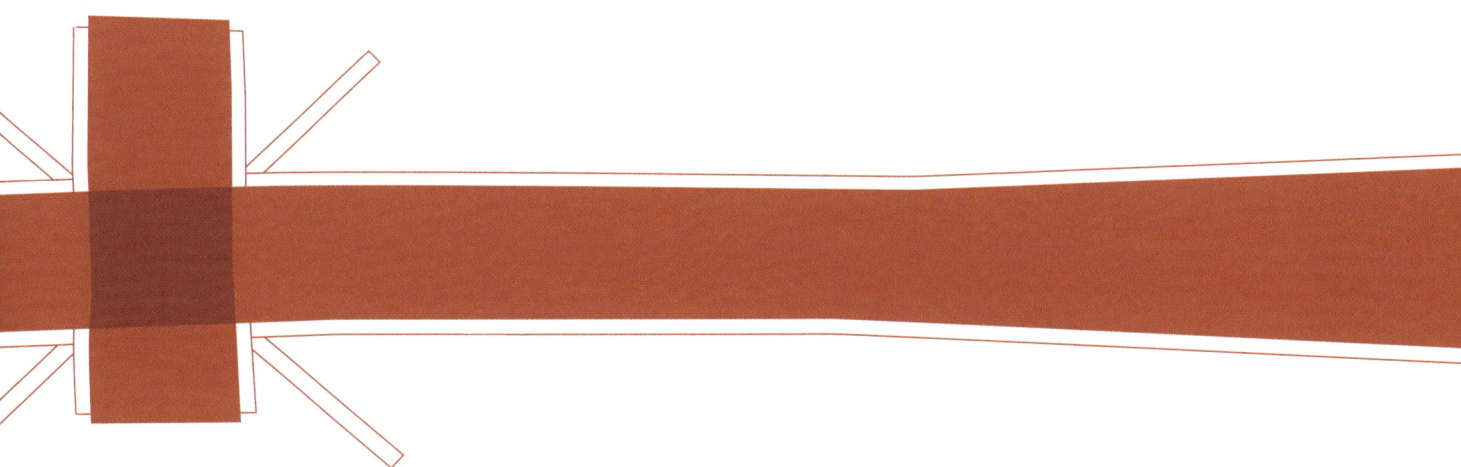

von
David Christie

Ernst Klett Verlag
Stuttgart · Leipzig

Kickoff Foundation
Workbook mit Lösungsheft

Autor: David Christie, Oxford

Werkübersicht:

Kickoff Foundation Schülerbuch, 978-3-12-808295-0
Kickoff Foundation Workbook mit Lösungsheft, 978-3-12-808303-2
Kickoff Upgrade Schülerbuch, 978-3-12-808296-7
Kickoff Upgrade Workbook mit Lösungsheft, 978-3-12-808304-9
Kickoff Lehrerhandbuch inkl. Digitalem Lehrer-Service mit Medien-DVD-ROM +
Lehrer-Audio-CDs (2), 978-3-12-808305-6

1. Auflage

1 9 8 7 6 5 | 29 28 27 26 25

Alle Drucke dieser Auflage sind unverändert und können im Unterricht nebeneinander verwendet werden.
Die letzte Zahl bezeichnet das Jahr des Druckes.

Redaktion: Gaby Bauer-Negenborn, Weßling
Herstellung: Sarah Ganser

Satz und Gestaltung: Satzkiste, Stuttgart
Umschlaggestaltung: KOMA AMOK, Kunstbüro für Gestaltung, Stuttgart
Reproduktion: Meyle + Müller Medien-Management, Pforzheim
Druck: Kern GmbH, Bexbach

Printed in Germany
ISBN 978-3-12-808303-2

Unit 1 At college

Grammar

1 's' or 'es'?

A Complete the table with the right forms of the verbs.

	to work	to go	to finish	to tidy*
I	work	go	finish	tidy
he/she/it	works			
we	work	go	finish	tidy
you	work	go	finish	tidy
they	work	go	finish	tidy

> **s!**
> He, she it – das 's' muss mit!
> Bei einigen Verben aber heißt
> das 'es'.

B Finish these sentences with the correct forms of the verbs in brackets (...).

1   She always _eats_____ (to eat) lunch at 12.30.

2   When Sam _____ (to finish) college, he _____ (to want) to be a hairdresser.

3   Jessica is an English businesswoman. She often _____ (to fly) to Germany on business trips.

4   In the evening, Adam _____ (to do) his homework, then he _____ (to watch) television.

5   George _____ (to like) football. He _____ (to play) every weekend in the football season.

6   William _____ (to study) hard all week but at the weekend he _____ (to relax).

7   My neighbour _____ (to wash) his car every Saturday.

2   **Ken, Marcie and Ella are students at two different community colleges in the USA. Read what they say below and on the next page and then complete the sentences about them.**

Hi. I'm Ken Kimura and I live in Seattle in the north-west of the United States. I'm a student at the Seattle City College and I'm on a media course. When I finish the course, I want to be a movie cameraman maybe in Hollywood. I go to college five days a week from 9 a. m. to 4 p. m.

→ * to tidy (a room): *(ein Zimmer) aufräumen*

We're Marcie DiMartino and Ella Harris. We live in Washington DC, the U.S. capital and we're students there at the Franklin D. Roosevelt Community College. We're on an IT course. When we finish, we both want to be computer technicians. We're best friends. We go to college together and we often hang out together at the weekend, too.

1 Ken Kamura _lives_____ in Seattle.

2 Marcie and Ella_____ in Washington DC.

3 When Ken _____ his course, he _____ to be a cameraman.

4 When Marcie and Ella _____ their course, they _____ to be computer technicians.

5 Ken _____ to college five days a week.

6 Marcie and Ella always _____ to college together – and they often _____ together at the weekend, too.

3 The *simple present* negative. The sentences below about Ken, Marcie and Ella are all false. Correct them.

1 Marcie and Ella live in Seattle

   _Marcie and Ella don't live in Seattle. They live in Washington DC._____

2 Ken lives in Washington DC.

   _____

3 Ken wants to be an IT technician.

   _____

4 Marcie and Ella want to work in the movie industry.

   _____

5 Marcie and Ella go to college separately*.

   _____

6 Ken goes to college two days a week.

   _____

7 Ken is a student at Franklin D. Roosevelt Community College.

   _____

8 Marcie and Ella are students at the Seattle City College.

   _____

_____

→ * separately: *getrennt, nicht zusammen*

4 The *simple present* questions. Read the text below, then make and
answer questions about Robin.

"Hi. My name's Robin and I live in England. I'm a student at a college in London. On a typical day, I get up at 6 o'clock and I go jogging. Then I have a shower, eat my breakfast, and I go to college on the underground. My first lesson starts at 9 o'clock and I finish at around 4.30. I get a lunch break from one until two. I often go into town and buy some fish and chips. When I come home, I do my homework in my room and then after supper at 6.30 I go on to the internet – Facebook normally. At the weekends, I have a part time job on Saturdays. I work in a supermarket. On Sundays, don't laugh (!), but I'm a very tidy person and on Sunday mornings I tidy my room."

1   Where <u>does</u> Robin <u>live</u>? (to live)

_<u>He lives in England.</u>_____

2   When _____ he _____? (to get up)

_____

3   How _____ he _____ to college? (to go)

_____

4   What _____? (he/to do/in his lunch break)

_____

5   Where _____? (he/to do/his homework)

_____

6   When _____? (he/to eat /his supper)

_____

7   Where _____? (he/to work/on Saturdays)

_____

8   What _____? (he/to do/on Sunday mornings)

_____

Vocabulary

5 Below are the names of some college courses. Match the halves.
Write down a German translation for each course.

Art and	Administration	_Kunst und Design_____
Automotive	Beauty	_____
Health and	Child Care	_____
Social Work and	Design	_____
Business	Mechanics	_____
Retail	Services	_____
Information	Technology	_____

6 Which preposition is right – *in*, *on* or *at*? Finish the sentences. All
the expressions were in the unit.

1 I'm a student _at_ a vocational college.

2 My college is _____ Germany.

3 There are three people _____ this picture.

4 Clyde, the student at KWCC, is _____ a business administration course.

5 His lessons start _____ 8.30 in the morning.

6 He plays sports _____ the afternoons.

7 And _____ the weekend, he hangs out with his friends.

8 There are 22 people _____ my class this year.

9 The oldest student _____ the moment is 75 years old.

7 Do the crossword. All the words and phrases were in the unit.

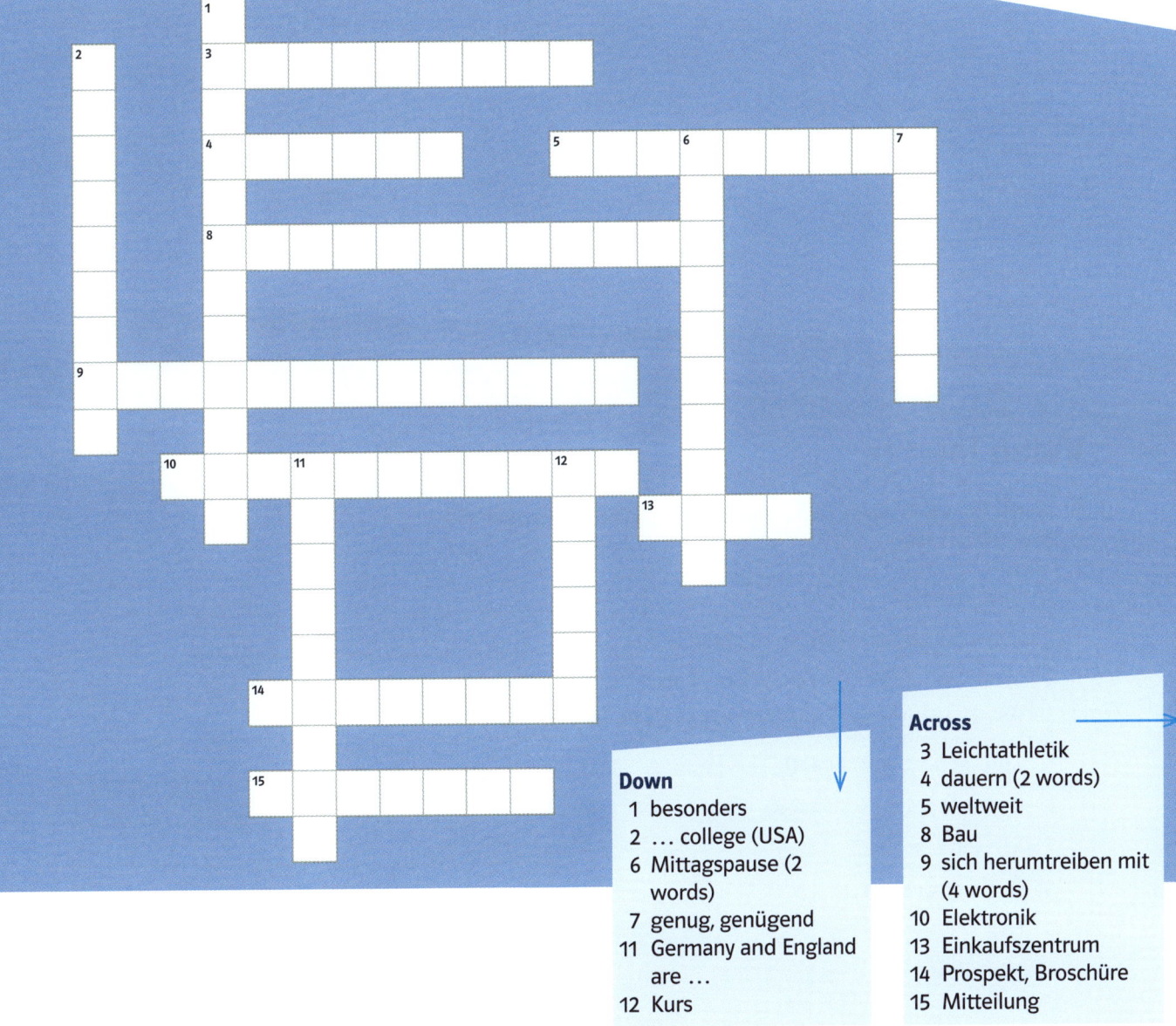

Down
1 besonders
2 … college (USA)
6 Mittagspause (2 words)
7 genug, genügend
11 Germany and England are …
12 Kurs

Across
3 Leichtathletik
4 dauern (2 words)
5 weltweit
8 Bau
9 sich herumtreiben mit (4 words)
10 Elektronik
13 Einkaufszentrum
14 Prospekt, Broschüre
15 Mitteilung

Writing

8 **You often write to an Amercian college student. Below is a typical, friendly email. Complete it with the correct phrases.**

Subject: my new college

(1) Hi _____ Abigal!

(2) _____ for your nice email last week. **(3)** _____ that your brother is OK again after the accident on his bike!

(4) _____ to tell you about my new college. I started there on Monday and it's really great. The other students in my classes seem nice and the lessons are so much more interesting than at school.

So how is your high school? **(5)** _____ all about it. When are your lessons? What are your favourite subjects? Who are your best friends?

(6) _____!

(7) _____

(8) (Your name) _____

Best wishes

~~Hi~~

Please write and tell me

I'm really glad

I'm writing today

Hoping to hear from you soon

Thanks very much

Video lounge

9 **Watch the video again. Write down the English phrases that you hear which mean ...**

1 Kein Problem! _____

2 nebenbei bemerkt (My name's Maria, ...) _____

3 in dieser Gegend (They show lots of musicals ...) _____

4 Was kann ich Ihnen bringen? (Restaurant) _____

5 Tagesgericht (Restaurant) _____

6 Guten Appetit! (Restaurant) _____

7 Ich wette _____

8 sich krank fühlen _____

9 Los! _____

10 Nie im Leben! _____

Unit 2 People and jobs

Grammar

1 Match the people and the jobs, then write sentences about the people.

Antonio

Dennis

Eve

and

Claire

Liam

Ed

Sarah   and

singer

shop assistant

 mechanic

fitness trainer

hairdresser

secretary

nursery assistant

1 Dennis _is a mechanic_____

2 Eve _____

3 Antonio _____

4 Sarah _____

5 Liam _____

6 Claire _____

7 Ed _____

✝ Vorsicht!

Im Englischen verwendest du 'a' (bzw. 'an') vor Berufen:
He is a mechanic.
He is mechanic.
I want to be an electrician.
I want to be electrician.

2 Write in the *–ing* forms of the verbs on the left. Be careful with some of the spellings (!).
Then finish the sentences on the right. Use the *simple present* or the *present continuous*.

1 to repair   _repairing_____
2 to serve (!)   _____
3 to cut (!)   _____
4 to write (!)   _____
5 to sing   _____
6 to play   _____
7 to help   _____

A Claire often _plays_____ with children.
   She _____ with some children now.
B Dennis often _____ cars in his job.
   He _____ a car at the moment.
C Antonio _____ hair right now.
   He _____ hair every day.
D Sarah _____ an email in this picture.
   She _____ lots of emails at work.

3 **Look back at the people on the last page again.**
Write sentences about *one* more person like the sentences in exercise 2.

_____

_____

_____

4 *Simple present* or *present continuous*? Finish the text about Martin with the correct forms of the verbs.

Martin Schuster **(1)** _lives_ (to live) in Cologne in Germany.

He **(2)** _____ (to be) a barman and he **(3)** _____

(to work) every day in the bar of a hotel in the city centre.

So what does Martin usually do in his job? Well, he **(4)** _____

(to bring) drinks to the customers in the bar. He often **(5)** _____

(to talk) to the customers too. And he **(6)** _____ (to wash)

glasses and **(7)** _____ (to clean*) the tables. In the photo,

it's 9 o'clock in the evening and Martin **(8)** _____ (to work)

at the moment. Right now, he **(9)** _____ (to bring) drinks to

some customers.

5 **Write *four* sentences about YOU.**
Write *two* things you often do and *two* things you're doing at the moment.

_____

_____

_____

_____

Vocabulary

6 **Here are some places where people work.**
Can you write the words?

1 RAB _bar_____

2 ANSLO _____

3 KARP _____

4 PORKSHOW _____

5 RUNRYES _____

6 ICEFOF _____

7 POSH _____

8 TENFISS BULC _____

──────

→ * to clean: *putzen*

7 Match the jobs and the job profiles below. Write in the jobs. Use your dictionary if necessary.

The A ... to Z of jobs

From architect to zoo worker there are hundreds of different jobs in the big world of work.

a telecom technician   a hairdresser

a sales representative   an IT technician   a journalist

a zoo worker   a secretary   a social worker

a plumber   a nurse   a (car) mechanic   a driver

a fitness trainer   ~~a fashion designer~~   a chef

a police officer   a bricklayer

a teacher   a bank employee

an architect

1 _A fashion designer_ designs clothes
2 _____ works in a kitchen
3 _____ cuts hair
4 _____ works in a hospital
5 _____ repairs cars
6 _____ designs buildings
7 _____ sells a company's products
8 _____ protects people, catches criminals etc.
9 _____ installs and repairs water pipes etc.
10 _____ builds houses and flats
11 _____ helps people with family problems etc.

12 _____ looks after animals
13 _____ works in a fitness club
14 _____ works in a school or college
15 _____ works in a bank
16 _____ installs and repairs telephones, cables etc.
17 _____ works for a newspaper or a magazine
18 _____ works in an office
19 _____ drives a lorry, a bus, a taxi etc.
20 _____ repairs and programs computers

8 **Read the tip box and complete the sentences with the correct words. Use your dictionary if you are not sure.**

after   forward to   ~~at~~   up   for

1 Wow! Look _at_____ that! It's a 1952 Cadillac!

2 – What are you doing, Jasmine?

   – I'm looking _____ my pen. I can't find it.

3 A nurse looks _____ patients in hospital.

4 If you don't know a word in English, you can

   look it _____ in a dictionary.

5 College finishes on 22 June. I'm looking _____

   _____ the last day!

Neue Verben bilden

Du kannst eine Menge neuer Verben im Englischen bilden, wenn du ein zweites (oder mehr) Wort/Wörter zu einem einfachen Verb hinzufügst. Beispielsweise gibt es *to get* = 'bekommen', aber es heißt *to get up* = 'aufstehen'. Mit einem dieser Verben ‚to look' gibt es sehr viele solcher Wortbildungen. Es entstehen eine Reihe neuer Verben, wenn du weitere Wörter hinzufügst.

9 **Do the crossword. All the words were in the unit.**

Across
1 the opposite of 22 across
4 the opposite of 'always'
5 Blume
6 a musical instrument
9 gewöhnlich
11 manchmal
13 a car mechanic works here
18 a man who works in a bar
19 a machine you find in a fitness club (2 words)
20 the opposite of 14 down
21 Diät
22 draußen

Down
2 the plural of 'story'
3 Kraftfahrzeug
7 freundlich
8 a dangerous reptile that lives in rivers
10 a country on the other side of the world
12 spring, …, autumn, winter
14 Süd-, südlich
15 sand near the sea
16 Kunde/Kundin
17 ungefähr
18 Schönheit

Writing

10 Describe the picture. There are some notes and some phrases to help you.
Look also at page 38 in your book. Write about 100 words.

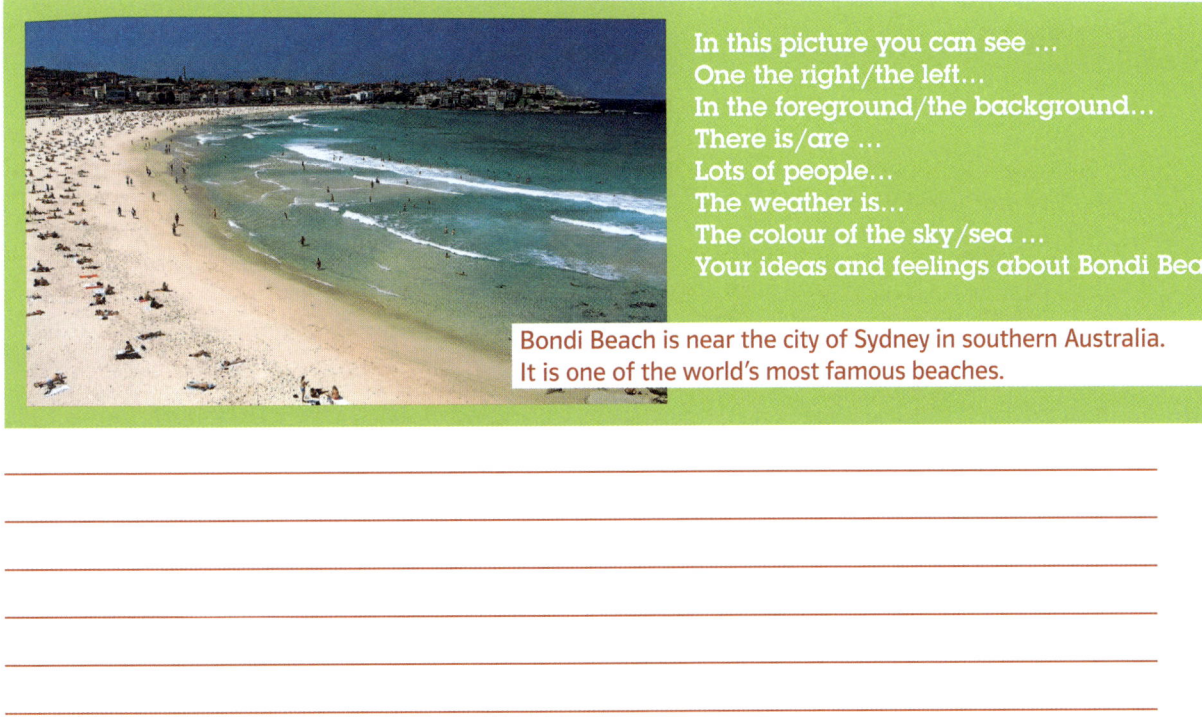

In this picture you can see …
One the right/the left…
In the foreground/the background…
There is/are …
Lots of people…
The weather is…
The colour of the sky/sea …
Your ideas and feelings about Bondi Beach

Bondi Beach is near the city of Sydney in southern Australia. It is one of the world's most famous beaches.

_____

_____

_____

_____

_____

_____

_____

_____

Video lounge

11 Watch the video and write in the missing phrases.

Sally   Good morning, **(1)** _how can I help you_ ?

John   Good morning. We're here to see Diane Kennedy **(2)** _____ .

Sally   **(3)** _____ , please?

John   Yes, it's John Carter and Paul Rogers from Australian Power Utilities. Here's my business card.

Sally   Thank you. I'll just call Ms Kennedy.

Paul   **(4)** _____ .

Sally   And can you complete these security forms, please?

Paul   Of course. **(5)** _____ , can I have a pen, please?

Sally   **(6)** _____ . Diane? I have Mr Rogers and Mr Carter in reception for you.

Right. Thank you.

Sally   Thank you. Please could you wear these visitors' badges? Someone will come down to get you in a

moment. **(7)** _____ .

Paul   Thanks.

John   **(8)** _____ .

Grammar

1 Match the expressions and the smileys. Write the letters A–D below.

A I don't like … (so much) / I'm not keen on … **B** I hate! **C** I love! **D** I (really) like …

1 _____ 2 _____ 3 _____ 4 _____

2 Verbs + *-ing*. Fill in the table with the *-ing*-forms of the verbs, then choose the best verbs to finish the sentences below. The two boxes on the right will help you.

1	watch	
2	do	
3	bake	
4	have	
5	shop	
6	sit	
7	veg	
8	play	
9	visit	
10	listen to	

I like doing …
Nach den Verben *to like / to love / to hate / to enjoy / to prefer* und Wendungen wie *to be keen on* steht häufig die *-ing*-Form:

I like **learning** English.
I'm not keen on **swimming**.

Die Schreibregeln bei den *-ing*-Formen beachten!
(→ Grammar 2: Verb + *-ing* Schreibregeln)

1 _____ in front of the telly means _____ on the sofa, _____ TV and _____ nothing!

2 His hobby is _____ cakes.

3 _____ nice friends is the most important thing for me.

4 My hobbies? Mmm, I like _____ the guitar and I love _____ music.

5 I like _____ my Grandma. She's old but she's still really funny.

6 I'm not keen on _____ – especially in supermarkets.

Denke daran:
You **watch** TV (the telly) and you **listen** to music.

I like **watching** TV in bed.
~~I like seeing TV …~~

She likes **listening to** music when she is doing her homework.
~~She likes hearing music …~~

3 The superlatives of adjectives. Below you can see some information about world records (the biggest, the most expensive, ...). First fill in the table with the superlatives of the adjectives, then choose the best superlatives to finish the records. Sometimes more than one answer is possible.

Adjective	Superlative	Adjective	Superlative
bad		high	
big		large	
dangerous		long	
expensive		old	
fast		rich	
happy		short	
heavy		strange	

Welcome to the Kickoff Book of Records!

1 **Rivers** The world's _____ river is the River Nile in Africa (6,600 km).

2 **Mountains** The _____ mountain in the world is Mount Everest.

3 **Trees** The _____ tree in the world is in California. It is over 5,000 years old.

4 **Animals** The world's _____ animals are cheetahs. They can run at an amazing 120 kilometres an hour. The _____ land animals are African elephants which weigh over 5 tonnes. The _____ bird is an ostrich. The _____ spiders are from South America. They are called 'Chaco Golden Knee' spiders and they are 22 cm across. And the _____ animals in the world – the ones which kill the most people every year? No, they're not tigers or lions or crocodiles. They're mosquitoes – they kill over 1 million people every year with malaria.

5 **Names** Sometimes parents give their children very unusual names. Some of the _____ names (this is true!) are: *boys*: Cheese, Daxx, Miggy, Panda, and Rocket, *girls*: Fairy, Moor, Kiwi, Tulip, Nyx and _____ of all: Zzyzx! In America, there are also some very funny names of towns. Among the _____ places are: Nothing, Arizona, Boring, Oregon, and No Name Colorado. The _____ place name is of a town in Wales in the UK. It is Llanfairpwllgwyngyllgogerychwyrndrobwllllantysiliogogogoch.

6 **Buildings** For many years, one of the world's _____ buildings was the Empire State Building in New York (443 metres with 102 floors). Today that seems quite small! The world's _____ building now is the Burj Khalifa Building in Dubai (830 metres with 163 floors).

7 **People and business** The world's _____ businessman is Bill Gates. He is personally worth $78 billion. The world's five _____ companies are Exxon (oil), Apple, Google, Wal-Mart (an American supermarket chain) and Bill Gates's company Microsoft.

High und tall
Das Wort *high* wird bei Bergen verwendet.
Das Wort *tall* steht bei Personen, Bäumen und Gebäuden.

8 **Literature** Most people agree that the _____ story ever was by the American writer Frederic Brown. In 1948 he wrote a science fiction story called Knock*. It has only 17 words. He imagines a world where everyone is dead – except one man. The story is: 'The last man on Earth sat alone in a room. There was a knock on the door.'

9 **That costs a lot of money!** If you want to buy some things, you have to pay a lot. The world's _____ bicycle comes from America and is made of gold. One bike costs $1,008,000. The _____ restaurant is on the holiday island of Ibiza. Only 12 people can eat there at one time and a meal costs 1,500 euros per person.

10 **Films** Some films are good, some are great, and some are absolutely terrible. Many critics agree that one of the _____ films ever made was the 1959 movie *Plan 9 from Outer Space*. The main actor died during the making of the film but the director continued with a different actor – who looked completely different!

11 **Countries** Every year, the UN (United Nations) makes a list of countries in which people are happy or sad. The ten _____ countries in 2014 (where life was best for the people there) were: Australia, Iceland, Austria, Finland, Canada, Sweden, The Netherlands, Switzerland, Norway and Denmark.

4 **The comparatives of adjectives. Use the information from exercise 3 to complete these sentences. Use the comparative forms of the adjectives.**

1 Mosquitoes kill more people a year than any other animal. They are much _____ (dangerous) than lions or tigers.

2 The Burj Khalifa Building in Dubai is much _____ (tall) than the older Empire State Building.

3 A golden bicycle is, of course, a lot _____ than an ordinary bike!

So small, but so dangerous! Mosquitoes kill over a million people a year.

4 You may think that some films are bad, but you can be sure that *Plan 9 from Outer Space* is _____! (bad)

5 People who live in countries like Australia or Switzerland are _____ (happy) than people who live in most other countries.

6 The River Amazon in South America is long, but the River Nile in Africa is a bit _____ (long).

7 Some children's names are much _____ (strange) than others. Cheese and ZZyzx, for example!

→ * knock: *Klopfen*

Vocabulary

5 Talking about sports and fitness. Look at the box on the right and the table below. Then finish the sentences with the correct forms of *to play*, *to do* or *to go*.

PLAY	football (soccer), tennis, table tennis, hockey, rugby, basketball, handball, golf badminton, video games, cards, chess
DO	karate, judo, yoga, athletics, aerobics, sports (in general)
GO	swimming, jogging, sailing, bowling, windsurfing, skateboarding, ice skating, snowboarding, cycling, skiing, fishing

Die Verben to play, to do und to go

I like going bowling with my friends.

Einige Sportarten stehen mit dem Verb *to play*, andere mit *to do* oder *to go*:
- *to play* a game (football, tennis, cards);
- *to do* an activity (karate, aerobics);
- *to go* often with verb + *-ing* (swimming, jogging).

1   In my free time I like _going_____ swimming.

2   Do you prefer _____ football or watching it on TV?

3   My favourite activity is doing karate but I like _____ yoga, too.

4   I'm not very keen on going cycling but I love _____ skateboarding.

5   I play table tennis at my youth club and I _____ aerobics there, too, twice a week.

6   My friend and I often _____ _____ ice skating at the weekend.

7   I'm not keen on _____ video games. I think they're boring.

8   How often do you _____ bowling? – About once a month.

9   I don't like _____ sports very much but I love _____ chess.

Writing

6 Write about your free time activities for your social networking page. The phrases below will help you. Write about 80–100 words.

In my free time	I like	playing football / baking cakes / …
I do that	(about)	once / twice / three times a week / (almost) every day / as often as I can / …
I do it		at home / at college / in town / in a club / at the gym / …
I like it	because	it's really interesting / it keeps me fit / I meet my friends / it's relaxing / …
I started	doing it	last year / two years ago / a long time ago / when I was small / …
One day	I would like to	become really good at it / play in a championship / beat all my friends at it / learn how to … / …

Video lounge

7 Arbeite zusammen mit einem Partner. Lest euch zuerst die Informationen zu den Filmtechniken durch. Schaut anschließend das Video an, unten links findet ihr das Filmskript dazu. Macht euch auf Deutsch Notizen zu den Techniken, die ihr erkennt und überlegt, welche Auswirkungen diese Techniken auf den Zuschauer haben. Notiert, was geschieht: Handlungen der Personen, Musik, Geräuscheffekte, Nahaufnahmen, Zeitlupeneinstellungen und alles andere, was euch auffällt.

Filmtechniken

Filme bestehen nicht nur aus Personen, die miteinander sprechen. Regisseure verwenden die verschiedensten Techniken, um …

- die Handlungen der Personen zu zeigen;
- über die Charaktere zu berichten;
- eine Atmosphäre von Spannung und Dramatik zu erzeugen;
- die Orte zu zeigen, an denen die Handlungen stattfinden.

Zu diesen Techniken gehören die Verwendung von Musik, Nahaufnahmen der Gesichter der Personen, Zeitlupeneinstellungen und Einstellungen der Szene, in der die Handlung stattfindet. Wenn ihr das nächste Mal einen Film oder ein Video anschaut, achtet mal auf diese Techniken. Es macht Spaß und ihr werdet viel besser verstehen, wie Filme und Videos funktionieren.

Go, Greg, go!
04:31

Eine Nahaufnahme von Gregs Gesicht. Sie macht die Szene dramatischer, weil man sich gut vorstellen kann, was Greg in diesem Moment denkt.

On the football field

Coach	OK, team, we've got a guest today, from England. Says he's a great offense player. He's going to be our fullback today.
Greg	Fullback?
Coach	Yeah, fullback. You just get the ball, carry the baby into the end zone. Or do the Brits play football differently? The team laugh. So let's show him what we can do. I write 32 on 2. Ready?
Team	Ready!
Player	Set! Hut! Hut!
Coach	Great job, defense! That's perfect tackling out there! Come on, let's get it done! Ah, let's give him another chance. You've got to run, Greg! Come on, let's do it again! Brits!
Greg	Brits never give up.
Player	Hut! Hut!
Cheerleaders	Offense go! Offense go! Offense go!

End: a photo of Greg, Maya, Josh and Carmen

Notizen

_____
_____
_____
_____
_____
_____
_____
_____
_____
_____
_____

Unit 4 Products and services

Grammar

1 Here is some more information about Mark Zuckerberg in a magazine article.
Complete the text with the verbs in brackets. Use the *simple past*. Be careful! Some verbs are negative.

Meet the world's youngest billionaire
Mark Zuckerberg, founder* and CEO of Facebook, is the world's youngest billionaire. How did he become so rich? We look at his life so far.

Mark Elliot Zuckerberg **(1)** __was born__ (to be born) in a small town in New York State on 14 May, 1984. His father **(2)** _____ (to be) a dentist and his mother a psychiatrist. Zuckerberg **(3)** _____ (to have) a normal and happy childhood but he **(4)** _____ (to be) special in one way: he **(5)** _____ (to love) computers and computer programming. He **(6)** _____ (to write) his first software at the age of 12, a program which his father **(7)** _____ (to use) in his dental practice. At high school, he **(8)** _____ (to invent) computer games. His programs **(9)** _____ (to be) so good that big internet companies like AOL and Microsoft **(10)** _____ (to offer**) to buy them and to give him a job. But Zuckerberg **(11)** _____ (not/to want) to work for a company – he **(12)** _____ (to like) writing his own software. After high school, Zuckerberg **(13)** _____ (to go) to one of America's most famous universities, Harvard, near Boston on the East Coast. There, he **(14)** _____ (to continue) to develop computer programs and soon all the students **(15)** _____ (to know) him and that he was clever with computers. In his second year (Americans call this the 'sophomore' year), he **(16)** _____ (to start) The Facebook with three college friends Dustin Moskovitz, Chris Hughes and Eduardo Saverin. It **(17)** _____ (to be) a social networking site for the students at Harvard. Students **(18)** _____ (can) upload their profiles and photos, and network with other students. Zuckerberg **(19)** _____ (not/to finish) his course. In 2004, he **(20)** _____ (to leave) Harvard to work full-time on his site. He **(21)** _____ (to change) the name to Facebook and at the end of 2004, the site **(22)** _____ (to have) 1 million users. Facebook **(23)** _____ (to grow) very quickly and in the following years more and more people – not just Harvard students but people worldwide – **(24)** _____ (to join). Again, big companies like Yahoo and MTV Network **(25)** _____ (to want) to buy the site. But again Zuckerberg **(26)** _____ (not/to want) to sell it. He still owns it today. Zuckerberg is now extremely rich, but he also believes that it is important for rich people to help others who don't have much money. In 2010, he **(27)** _____ (to give) $100 million dollars to build better schools in New Jersey. Also in that year, he **(28)** _____ (to promise***) to give 50% of all his money in future to help poor people.

_____

→ * founder: *Gründer*   → ** to offer: *anbieten*   → *** to promise: *versprechen*

2 Here are some Quick Facts about pizzas.
Make questions about the text and answer them.

Pizza: Quick Facts

First pizzas
People all around the Mediterranean* ate flat bread hundreds, even thousands of years ago.

First modern pizzas
A round flat bread like a pizza was popular with poor people in the town of Naples, Italy, in the 1800s. A baker in the town called Raffaele Esposito, made the first pizza like those we eat today in 1889. It was for the Italian Queen Margharita. He used (red) tomatoes, (white) mozzarella cheese and (green) basil** – the Italian flag is red, white and green. The queen loved it and the baker became famous.

Pizzas in the USA
The first pizzas came to New York in 1905 when an Italian called Gennaro Lombardi opened the first pizzeria there. But pizzas only became popular all across America after World War II. Lots of American soldiers ate pizzas during the war in Italy and wanted to have them at home.

Pizzas in Germany
Another Italian, Nicola di Camillo, opened Germany's first pizzeria in Wurzburg in 1952.

1 Where _did_____ people _eat_____ (to eat) the first flat bread?

They _____ it all around the Mediterranean.

2 When _____ an Italian baker _____ (to make) the first

modern pizza?

He _____ it in _____ .

3 What colours _____ he _____ (to use)?

He _____

4 Why _____ he _____ (to use) these colours?

_____

5 Where _____ (Gennaro Lombardi/to open) the first American pizzeria?

_____

6 When _____ (pizzas/to become) popular all across the USA?

_____

7 Where and when _____ (another Italian/to open) Germany's first pizzeria?

_____

_____

_____
→ * Mediterranean: *Mittelmeer*   →** basil: *Basilikum*

3 In this crossword puzzle, all the answers are the *simple past* forms of irregular verbs. Just write in the *simple past* of the verb which is the clue.

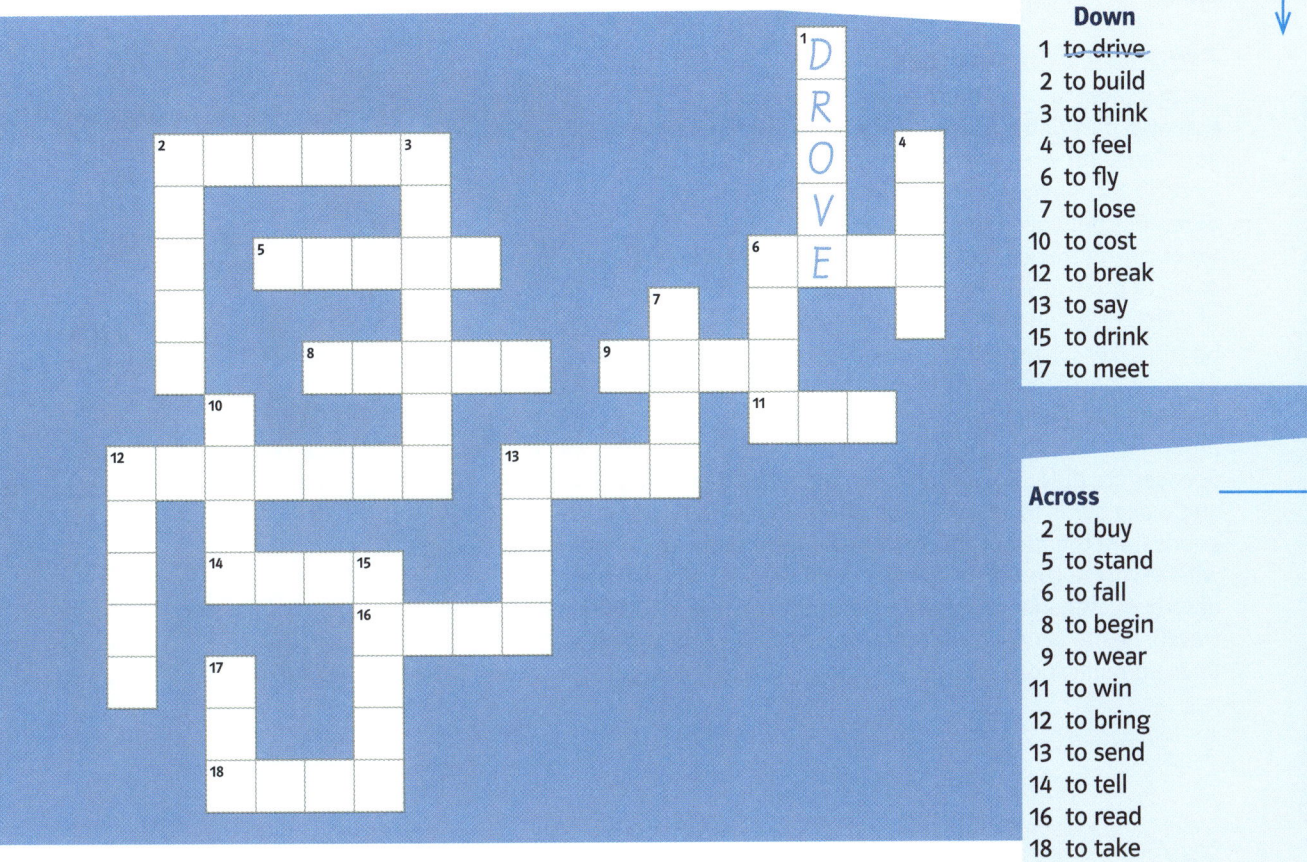

Down

1 to drive
2 to build
3 to think
4 to feel
6 to fly
7 to lose
10 to cost
12 to break
13 to say
15 to drink
17 to meet

Across

2 to buy
5 to stand
6 to fall
8 to begin
9 to wear
11 to win
12 to bring
13 to send
14 to tell
16 to read
18 to take

Vocabulary

4 Look at the tips box, then finish the sentences below with *in, last, on* or *ago*.

1 Mark Zueckerberg was born _on_____ 14 May, 1984.

2 Adi and Rudolf Dassler started their sports shoe company
_____ 1924.

3 What did you do _____ weekend?

4 I started lerning English about 10 years _____ .

5 Did you know? _____ the 1970s, a mobile phone cost
around $4,000!

6 _____ year, we went to London for our holidays.

7 _____ Tuesday last week, we did an important class test
in English.

+ **Zeitangaben mit dem *simple past***

Das *simple past* wird oft mit folgenden Zeitangaben verwendet:

in *the 1960s, the Sixties, 2011, 1986*
Vorsicht! *in* muss immer mit Jahreszahlen verwendet werden!
*He was born **in** 1998.*
He was born 1998.

last *week, month, Tuesday, weekend, year*

on *3 April (1990)*
Friday (last week)

ago *a week **ago**, two years **ago***
Vorsicht! *ago* steht am Ende der Zeitangabe!

5 **Read the short text, then write words into the mindmap below. Think of these words yourself – use your dictionary if necessary. There are gaps for 12 words in the mindmap, but you can write in more!**

Products and services

We buy them and use them every day. They are an essential part of the economy. And you learn about them at college. But what are products (sometimes also called 'goods') and services and most important, what is the difference between them?

Products are things. You can see them and you can hold many of them in your hands. There are, of course, millions of different products but we can put them into categories (groups). For example there are household products like washing machines and furniture; food products; beauty products like shampoo and make-up; and electronic products.

Services are different. You can't see them but they help us every day and make our lives easier. Shops provide* retail services – they bring goods from the manufacturer to shops (real shops or online shops) where we, the customers can buy them. Again, there are many different categories of services. Transport services (which help us to travel); health services; education services (like your college); and telecommunications services are just some examples.

We use retail services every day when we buy things – either in shops and supermarkets or online.

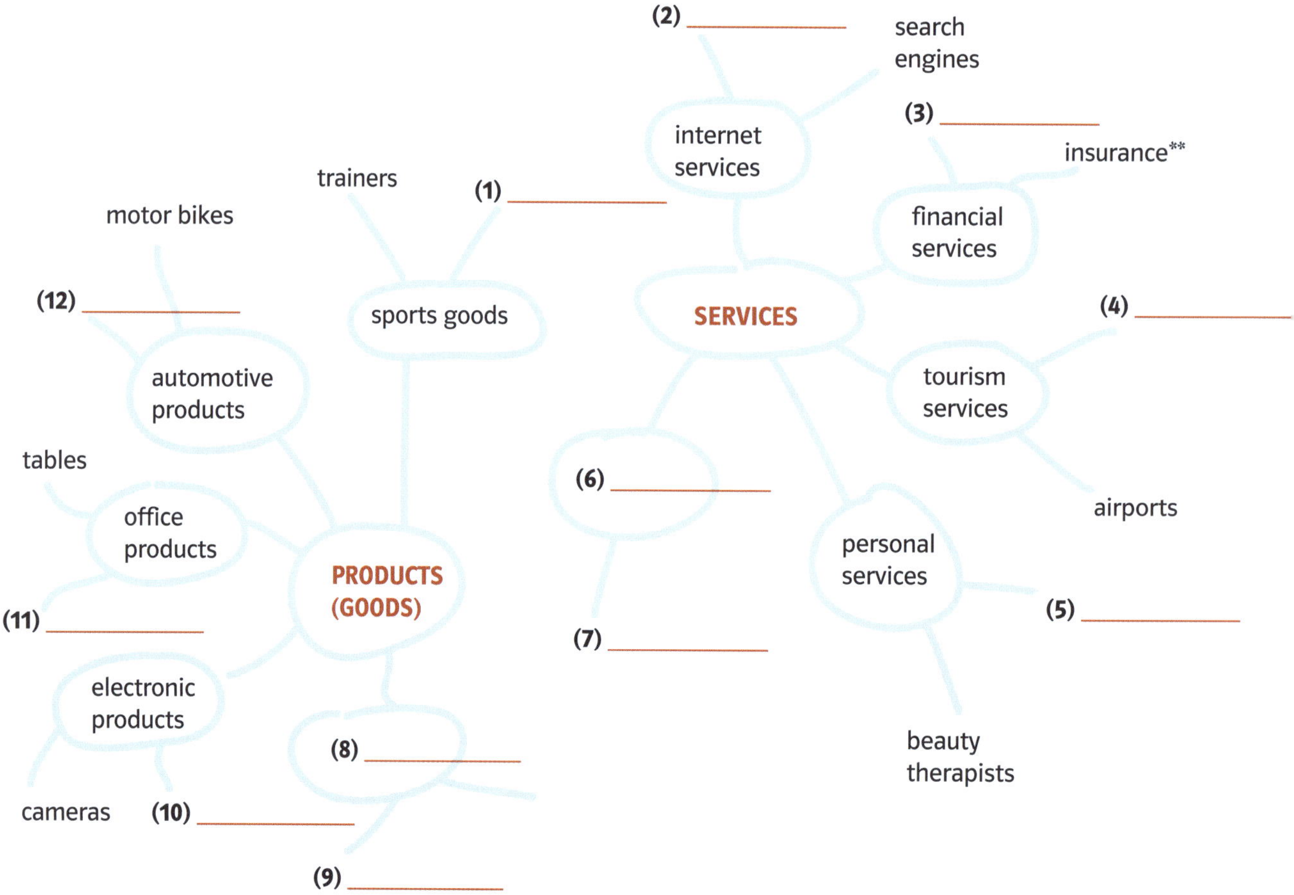

(2) _____   search engines

(3) _____

internet services   (1) _____   insurance**

trainers   financial services

motor bikes   SERVICES   (4) _____

(12) _____   sports goods

automotive products   tourism services

tables   (6) _____   airports

office products   PRODUCTS (GOODS)   personal services   (5) _____

(11) _____   (7) _____

electronic products   beauty therapists

(8) _____

cameras   (10) _____

(9) _____

→ * to provide: *bieten, liefern*   → ** insurance: *Versicherung*

Writing

6 **Write about 100 words about the products that you own* and the services you use.**

I own a number of products. At home I have _____

For college, I have _____

I also own _____

The product which I like best/My favourite product is _____ because

_____

I got this product (when?) _____

I use a lot of different services every day. Among them are _____

_____

The service which is most important to me is _____ because

_____

I started using this service (when?) _____

Video lounge

7 **At the beginning of the video, Greg, Josh and Maya are in a scene in a Western movie. Below is the script for the scene. Listen and write in the missing words and phrases. (You could act out the scene in class!)**

Josh is standing in a saloon. He looks up. Greg comes down the stairs.

Josh   She's mine. (1) _____ .

Maya is sitting at a table. She looks at the two men, worried.

Greg   Her. Never.

Maya   (2) _____ . There must be another way.

Josh   You know there isn't. You must have seen this coming. All these years living, travelling,

(3) _____ . It was always the three of us.

Greg   This is nothing for a real man. It's either him or me. I don't like to share.

Maya stands up quickly. She goes to Greg.

Maya   No! (4) _____ .

Greg pushes Maya away. She goes to Josh.

Maya   Please don't hurt each other. (5) _____ the both of you.

Josh   No.

He pushes Maya away.

Josh   *To Greg.* It can't be this way.

Greg   Go ahead. (6) _____ .

They fight. Greg hits Josh and he falls over the table. Josh gets up. He has a gun in his hand.

Maya   No!

The two men look at each other. Josh fires the gun and hits Greg in the shoulder. Greg falls to the ground.

―――
→ * to own: *besitzen*

Grammar

1 **Below are some sentences about four very different jobs. Complete the sentences.**
Use *must* or *has/have (to do)* and the verbs in brackets.

Firefighters with their fire engine

A social worker

A web designer

A glazier

1 Firefighters put out* fires. They __must be__ (must/to be)
   fit and strong. They also often _____ (to have/to drive)
   very quickly to the fire.

2 Social workers help people. A social worker _____
   (to have/to communicate) well with people and _____
   (must/to understand) their problems.

3 Web designers _____ (to have/to be) clever with
   computers and they _____ (must/to be) creative and
   have good design ideas.

4 A glazier cuts and installs glass – in windows, for example.
   A glazier _____ (to have/to like) working with her or
   his hands and _____ (must/to be) very careful at
   work – no-one wants a broken window!

✝ *Must* **und**
has/have (to do)
Die Verben *must* und *have*
(to do) können beide mit
der Bedeutung ‚müssen'
verwendet werden, aber pass
auf, denn es gibt ein paar
wichtige Unterschiede bei
ihrer Verwendung.
Must
• bleibt bei allen Personen
  gleich
• Auf *must* folgt der Infinitiv
  ohne *to*: I must *go* now.
Have (to do)
• In der dritten Person musst
  du *has* verwenden.
• Auf *have/has (to do)* folgt
  der Infinitiv **mit** *to*: I have
  to go now.

→ * to put out a fire: *(ein Feuer) löschen*

2 *Mustn't* means 'nicht dürfen'. You're in your town in Germany with a friend from America – who doesn't speak German. You see these signs and your friend wants to know what they mean. Explain in English. There are some words and phrases to help you with some of the signs.

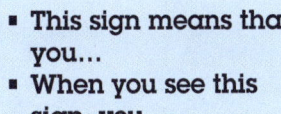

A – Hier bitte nicht spielen
B – Fahrräder abstellen verboten!
C – Wir warten draußen!
D – Bitte den Rasen nicht betreten!
E – BADEN VERBOTEN
F
G – Skateboard fahren verboten!

- This sign means that you…
- When you see this sign, you…

- to leave (a bicycle)
- to bring a dog (into a shop)
- ‚der Rasen‘: the grass/the lawn
- to skateboard

A   This sign means that you _____ (here).

B   _____

C   _____

D   _____

E   _____

F   _____

G   _____

3 *Must/has (to do)* or *doesn't have (to do)*? Complete the texts about Faith and Connie below and on the next page.

Faith
office worker

Faith lives in Phoenix, Arizona. She's an office worker. She **(1)** _has to_ work every day from 9 a.m. to 5 p.m. At work, she **(2)** _____ wear smart clothes and she **(3)** _____ be polite with her boss and her firm's customers. Sometimes she **(4)** _____ work on Saturdays, too. But she **(5)** _____ work on Sundays – that's always her free day.

Connie is a student at a college in Phoenix. She **(6)** _____ work in an office every day from 9 a.m. to 5 p.m. But she **(7)** _____ go to college from Monday to Friday. At college she usually wears jeans – she **(8)** _____ wear smart clothes like Faith. So is Connie's life easy? No! She **(9)** _____ do lots of tests and exams and they're hard!

Connie
student

Vocabulary

4 **Complete the word puzzle. The answer is often a phrase with more than one word. All the expressions were in your book on page 53. Then use expressions from the puzzle to finish the sentences a-e below.**

Across
1 im Brandfall
2 Gabelstapler
3 Gefahr
4 unbeaufsichtigt
5 … site = Baustelle
6 Achtung!
7 Gehörschutz
8 nasser Boden
9 Schutzbrille
10 Sicherheit
11 Betreten verboten

a   _____ protect your eyes.

b   You must wear _____ when there is a lot of loud noise.

c   Please do not leave your baggage _____ .

d   You mustn't go into that room. The sign says: _____ .

e   _____ , break the glass and ring the fire alarm.

5 **Workplace English. Here are some people at work. Look at the pictures.**

a First find the job titles and the name of the workplace for each picture and complete the table below the pictures.

b Then find and write in the missing words A-O in the pictures. Use your dictionary if necessary.

electrician

construction worker

~~office worker(s)~~

a journalist

doctor's receptionist

doctor's practice

an IT technician

house

~~office~~

construction site

	JOB TITLE	WORKPLACE
PICTURE 1	office worker(s)	office
PICTURE 2		
PICTURE 3		
PICTURE 4		

computer keyboard   desk   T-shirt   work boots

           tools   wheelbarrow   patient

computers   hard hat   reception desk

    concrete mixer   lamps   telephone   office chair

                                   step ladder

Writing

6 Next month, two students from America will spend two weeks at your college. Write some rules for them – tell them some important things they must or mustn't do. There are some ideas below to help you but you can think of other ideas yourself.

smoking

mobile phones

clothes

class tests

food and drink

lesson times

classrooms

teachers

homework

books/pens/notebooks etc.

bikes/cars/motor bikes

STUDENTS HERE MUST:

1 _____

2 _____

3 _____

WE MUSTN'T:

1 _____

2 _____

3 _____

Video lounge

7 Watch the video and write in the missing words and phrases.

Jasmine Here we are. Can I take **(1)** _____ ?

John Thank you.

Jasmine Would you like to sit down? I'm afraid Diane is **(2)** _____ .
Would you like a cup of coffee?

John Er . . .

Jasmine Or **(3)** _____ .

John I think I'd like some coffee, please.

Jasmine Would you like **(4)** _____ ?

John Yes, please. Both. Thanks.

Jasmine And how about you, Mr Rogers?

Paul Please call me Paul. I'd like **(5)** _____ , please.

Jasmine Here you are, Paul.

Paul Thanks very much.

Jasmine **(6)** _____ , but Diane should be here soon.

John That's fine. Don't worry.

Kickoff Foundation
Workbook mit Lösungsheft

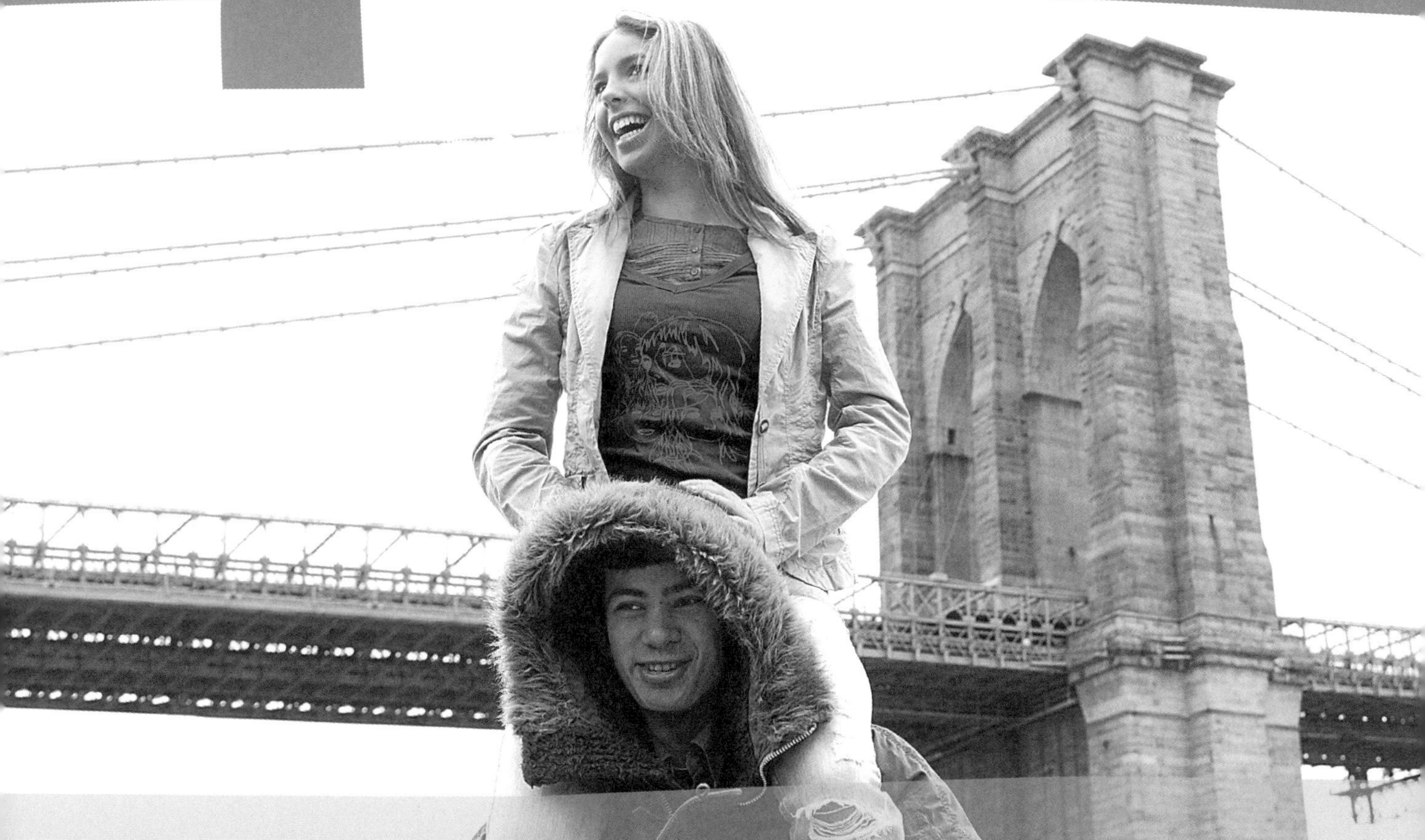

Lösungen

Unit 1: At college

Grammar

1 a goes, finishes, tidies

    2 finishes / wants
    3 flies
    4 does / watches
    5 likes / plays
    6 studies / relaxes
    7 washes

2   2 live
    3 finishes / wants
    4 finish / want
    5 goes
    6 go / hang out

3   2 Ken doesn't live in Washington DC. He lives in Seattle.
    3 Ken doesn't want to be an IT technician. He wants to be a cameraman.
    4 Marcie and Ella don't want to work in the movie industry. They want to be computer technicians.
    5 Marcie and Ella don't go to college separately. They (always) go (to college) together.
    6 Ken doesn't go to college two days a week. He goes (to college) five days a week.
    7 Ken isn't a student at Franklin D. Roosevelt College. He's a student at the Seattle City College.
    8 Marcie and Ella aren't students at the Seattle City College. They're students at Franklin D. Roosevelt College.

4   2 When does he get up?
      He gets up at 6 o'clock.
    3 How does he go to college?
      He goes to college on the underground.
    4 What does he do in his lunch break?
      He (often) goes to town and buys some fish and chips.
    5 Where does he do his homework?
      He does his homework in his room.
    6 When does he eat his supper?
      He eats his supper at 6.30.
    7 Where does he work on Saturdays?
      He works in a supermarket (on Saturdays).
    8 What does he do on Sunday mornings?
      He tidies his room (on Sunday mornings).

Vocabulary

5 (Art and Design), Automotive Mechanics, Health and Beauty, Social Work and Child Care, Business Administration, Retail Services, Information Technology.

(Kunst und Design), Fahrzeugmechanik, Gesundheits- und Schönheit(spflege), Sozialarbeit und Kinderbetreuung, Betriebswirtschaftslehre, Einzelhandelsdienstleistungen, Informatik

6   2 in   6 in
    3 in   7 at
    4 on   8 in
    5 at   9 at

7

Down	Across
1 particularly	3 athletics
2 community	4 to last
6 lunch break	5 worldwide
7 enough	8 construction
11 countries	9 to hang out with
12 course	10 electronics
	13 mall
	14 brochure
	15 message

Writing

  2 Thanks very much
  3 I'm really glad
  4 I'm writing today
  5 Please write and tell me
  6 Hoping to hear from you soon
  7 Best wishes
  8 (your name)

Video lounge

  1 No problem!
  2 by the way
  3 (a)round here
  4 What can I get you?
  5 (the) special
  6 Enjoy!
  7 I bet
  8 to feel sick
  9 Go!
  10 No way!

Unit 2: People and jobs

Grammar

1 2 is a shop assistant.
3 is a hairdresser.
4 is a secretary.
5 is a singer.
6 is a nursery assistant.
7 is a fitness trainer.

2 2 serving
3 cutting
4 writing
5 singing
6 playing
7 helping

A is playing
B repairs, is repairing
C is cutting, cuts
D is writing, writes

3 *Mögliche Lösung*
Liam often sings in clubs. He is singing (He's singing) in a club right now.
Ed often helps people in his fitness club. He is helping a woman now.
Eve often serves customers in her shop. She is serving a customer at the moment.

4 2 is
3 works
4 brings
5 talks
6 washes
7 cleans
8 is working
9 is bringing

5 *Mögliche Lösung*
I often play football at the weekends.
I often hang out with my friends in the afternoons.
I'm sitting in my room at home at the moment.
I'm doing this exercise in my workbook.

Vocabulary

6 2 salon
3 park
4 workshop
5 nursery
6 office
7 shop
8 fitness club

7 2 a chef
3 a hairdresser
4 a nurse
5 a (car) mechanic
6 an architect
7 a sales representative
8 a police officer
9 a plumber
10 a bricklayer
11 a social worker
12 a zoo worker
13 a fitness trainer
14 a teacher
15 a bank employee
16 a telecom technician
17 a journalist
18 a secretary
19 a driver
20 an IT technician

8 2 for
3 after
4 up
5 forward to

	Across		**Down**	
9	1 inside		2 stories	
	4 never		3 vehicle	
	5 flower		7 friendly	
	6 guitar		8 crocodile	
	9 usually		10 Australia	
	11 sometimes		12 summer	
	13 workshop		14 southern	
	18 barman		15 beach	
	19 exercise machine		16 customer	
	20 northern		17 around	
	21 diet		18 beauty	
	22 outside			

Writing

10 *Mögliche Lösung*
In this picture you can see Bondi Beach. It is a famous beach near Sydney is southern Australia. On the left you can see the beach and on the right you can see the sea. In the background there are some buildings. Lots of people are sitting or lying on the beach. The weather is warm and sunny and the people are all wearing swimming costumes. The sky is dark blue and the sea is blue and green. There are also some white waves. I think Bondi Beach looks a lovely place. I would like to go there!
(98 words)

Video lounge

11 2 at 10 o'clock.
   3 Can I have your names
   4 Thank you
   5 Excuse me
   6 Here you are
   7 Please have a seat
   8 OK

Unit 3: Free time

Grammar

1 B – A – D – C

2
1 watching	1 Vegging, sitting,
2 doing	watching, doing
3 baking	2 baking
4 having	3 Having
5 shopping	4 playing, listening to
6 sitting	5 visiting
7 vegging	6 shopping
8 playing	
9 visiting	
10 listening to	

3 bad – the worst
   big – the biggest
   dangerous – the most dangerous
   expensive – the most expensive
   fast – the fastest
   happy – the happiest
   heavy – the heaviest
   high – the highest
   large – the largest
   long – the longest
   old – the oldest
   rich – the richest
   short – the shortest
   strange – the strangest

   1 longest
   2 highest
   3 oldest
   4 fastest, heaviest, biggest, biggest, most dangerous
   5 strangest, strangest, funniest, longest
   6 tallest, tallest
   7 richest, biggest
   8 shortest
   9 most expensive, most expensive
   10 worst
   11 happiest

4
1 more dangerous	5 happier
2 taller	6 longer
3 more expensive	7 stranger
4 worse	

Vocabulary

5 2 playing
   3 doing
   4 going
   5 do
   6 go
   7 playing
   8 go
   9 doing, playing

Writing

6 *Mögliche Lösung*
   In my free time I like playing hockey. I do that two or three times a week and almost every weekend. I do it together with my best friends from school in a club. We play field hockey outdoors in summer and indoor hockey in the gym in winter. I like doing sports because it keeps me fit and I can meet my friends. I started doing it a long time ago when I was only five years old. One day I would like to play in a big championship. But that's not very realistic, it's only a dream!
   (99 words)

7 • *dramatische Musik (erzeugt Spannung / Dramatik)*
   • *Herzklopfen (Gregs Angst vor dem Spiel)*
   • *Nahaufnahme von Gregs Gesicht (man kann seine Gefühle ahnen)*
   • *Zeitlupe während Greg sich zum Spielen fertigmacht (erzeugt Spannung)*
   • *Spieler rennen auf die Kamera zu (man sieht die Szene aus Gregs Perspektive)*
   • *Greg rennt mit dem Ball und wird mehrmals angegriffen (die „Geschichte" der Szene)*
   • *Musik während Greg mit dem Ball rennt (gibt das Gefühl der Wiederholung der Handlung)*
   • *Maya oder andere Personen (man sieht ihre Reaktionen auf die Handlung)*
   • *Greg rennt am Ende mit dem Ball und wird von den anderen Spieler hochgehoben (die „Geschichte" der Szene)*
   • *Foto am Ende: Das Spiel ist vorbei, alle sind glücklich. Greg, Maya und Josh werden immer an das Spiel und an ihre Reise in die USA denken.*

Unit 4: Products and services

Grammar

1
2	was	11	didn't want	20	left
3	had	12	liked	21	changed
4	was	13	went	22	had
5	loved	14	continued	23	grew
6	wrote	15	knew	24	joined
7	used	16	started	25	wanted
8	invented	17	was	26	didn't want
9	were	18	could	27	gave
10	offered	19	didn't finish	28	promised

2
1 ate
2 did / make / made / 1889
3 did / use / used (the colours) red, white and green
4 did / use / He used them because the Italian flag is red, white and green.
5 did Gennaro Lombardi open / He opened it in New York.
6 did pizzas become / They became popular (all across America) after World War II.
7 did another Italian open / He opened it in Wurzburg in 1952.

3

Down		**Across**	
(1	drove)	2	bought
2	built	5	stood
3	thought	6	fell
4	felt	8	began
6	flew	9	wore
7	lost	11	won
10	cost	12	brought
11	broke	13	sent
13	said	14	told
15	drank	16	read
17	met	18	took

Vocabulary

4
2 in
3 last
4 ago
5 In
6 Last
7 On

5 *Mögliche Lösung*
1 a football
2 social media websites
3 banks
4 travel agents
5 hairdressers
6 (tele)communications services
7 mobile phone companies
8 household products
9 fridges
10 televisions
11 chairs
12 cars

Writing

6 *Mögliche Lösung*
I own a number of products. At home, I have a computer and a DVD player. For college, I have a calculator and pens and pencils. I also own a bike and a skateboard. My favourite product is my smartphone because I can keep in touch with friends and take photos. I got it last year. I use a lot of different services every day. Among them are a hairdresser, buses and the S-Bahn in my town and, of course, shops. The service which is most important to me is the social networking site Facebook because I always know about my friends and I can post and look at photos. I started using this service two years ago.
(118 words)

Video lounge

7
1	Forget her	4	Maybe we can live together
2	Please stop it		
3	working together	5	I love
		6	Make my day

Unit 5: Dos and dont's at work

Grammar

1
1 have to drive
2 has to communicate, must understand
3 have to be, must be
4 has to like, must be

2 *Mögliche Lösung*
A mustn't play football (here).
B This sign means that you mustn't leave bicycles here.
C This sign means that you mustn't bring your dog into the shop.
D When you see this sign, you know that you mustn't walk on the grass.
E This sign means that you mustn't swim here.
F When you see this sign, you know that you mustn't eat or drink.
G This sign means that you mustn't skateboard here.

3
2	has to / must	6	doesn't have to
3	has to / must	7	has to / must
4	has to / must	8	doesn't have to
5	doesn't have to	9	has to / must

Vocabulary

4
1	in case of fire	a	goggles
2	fork lift truck	b	ear protectors
3	danger	c	unattended
4	unattended	d	keep out
5	construction	e	in case of fire
6	caution		
7	ear protectors		
8	wet floor		
9	goggles		
10	security		
11	keep out		

5 a PICTURE 2 electrician, house
PICTURE 3 doctor's receptionist, doctor's practice
PICTURE 4 construction worker, construction site

b
A	computers	I	patient
B	telephone	J	reception desk
C	desk	K	computer keyboard
D	office chair	L	hard hat
E	lamps	M	work boots
F	T-shirt	N	concrete mixer
G	tools	O	wheelbarrow
H	step ladder		

Writing

6 *Mögliche Lösung*
MUST
1 wait outside the classroom until the teacher arrives
2 bring pens, notebooks etc. to all lessons
3 arrive punctually for lessons

MUSTN'T
1 smoke in the college
2 use mobile phones in lessons
3 eat or drink in lessons

Video lounge

7
1 your coat
2 still in a meeting
3 a glass of water or juice
4 milk and sugar
5 some orange juice
6 I'm sorry you have to wait

Unit 6: Success stories

Grammar

1
2 Dan is an office worker. He has worked for the company since 2010.
3 Michael is a warehouse worker. He has worked for the company since 2008.
4 Carolyn is a manager. She has worked for the company for four years.
5 Mrs Ellis is a receptionist. She has worked for the company for a long time!

2 *Mögliche Lösung*
1 How long have you been with the firm, Dan?
I've been with them since 2010.
2 How long have you been with the firm, Carolyn?
I've been with them for four years.

3
2	done	2	has sold
3	drunk	3	has worn
4	driven	4	has driven
5	gone	5	has made
6	had	6	has known
7	known		
8	made		
9	sold		
10	sung		
11	spent		
12	worn		

4
2	came	16	were
3	lived	17	were
4	was born	18	could
5	moved	19	loved
6	has lived	20	wanted
7	grew up	21	had
8	went	22	sold
9	had	23	started
10	worked	24	has run
11	left	25	has grown
12	went	26	employed
13	studied	27	married
14	worked	28	have had
15	saw		

Vocabulary

5
2 unsuccessful	2 irregular
3 irregular	3 impossible
4 to disagree	4 unemployed
5 impossible	5 disagree
6 unfriendly	6 disadvantages
7 to dislike	
8 disadvantage	
9 imperfect	
10 uncomfortable	
11 unemployed	
12 unusual	

6
Down	**Across**
1 favourite	4 unemployed
2 famous	5 unsuccessful
3 success story	8 disk jockey
6 firm	10 earn
7 reporter	14 different
9 employee	15 dyslexic
11 friendly	16 plumber
12 wife	18 Poland
13 children	19 maybe
17 local	20 marry

7 *Mögliche Lösung*
(an, and, another, ago), at, age, art, can, came, come, comes, cash, course, day, days, daily, dear, destroy, dirty, dog, dogs, dot, ever, every, fat, fog, fast, famous, film, film star, firm, five, find, give, gave, gives, get, gets, got, ghost, game, games, gone, go, had, have, halt, hand, has, hard, hand, her, in, hit, hits, lesson, leave, leaves, left, lost, long, lady, last, man, men, made, March, most, more, meet, meets, move, moves, moved, must, never, name, names, nil, noise, noisy, not, no, over, out, outside, or, on, other, others, old, race, run, runs, ran, read, reads, red, see, sees, say, says, sand, sort, said, she, seem, seems, sail, sailor, story, stories, stay, stays, sing, sings, sang, singer, should, shoulder, strange, tree, three, today, time, toy, the, these, those, uncle, undo, under, very, voice, yes, year

Writing

8 (Today I want to write to you about the place where I live. It's called) X (and I have lived here since) I was born. It is quite a big town with around 40,000 inhabitants. The town is partly old and partly modern. The oldest buildings are the town hall and a church in the centre of town. Among the new buildings are a big shopping centre and a new sports centre. The town isn't industrial but there are lots of modern businesses here. In the centre of town there is a famous statue of a woman on a horse. My favourite place in town is High Street because there are lots of small cafés here where I meet my friends. My town isn't particularly exciting but I like it because it is quite pretty and the people here are friendly.
(120 words)

Video lounge

9
1 Nice to meet you
2 Nice to meet you, too
3 This is my colleague
4 I'm very sorry I'm late
5 meeting
6 don't worry

Unit 7: Looking ahead

Grammar

1
2 They are going to organise it in the college sports hall.
3 They had a disco (last year).
4 They are going to have a live band (this year).
5 She is going to contact some guys in a band.
6 At midnight, they are going to show a movie.

2 *Mögliche Lösung*
We are going to have the party on the riverside. We're not going to play loud music because of the people living near by. But we're going to bring a guitar, so we can make our own music and sing along. We're going to have a barbecue and maybe we can have a campfire, too. And the best thing: we're going to go swimming at midnight!

3
1 Sentence B: George won't die when he's 30. Something bad will happen and his life will be hard for two or three years.
2 Sentence D: George's best job won't be his second job. He won't have that job very long. His best job will be the third.
3 Sentence F: All George's children won't be boys, they'll all be girls.

Vocabulary

4
1 ahead	5 up
2 after	6 out
3 forward to	7 at
4 for	

5

Down		Across	
1	area	2	shower
3	washbasin	7	houseplant
4	dining table	8	wall
5	entrance	9	pinboard
6	clock	10	cupboard
11	paint	12	sink
13	kettle	14	microwave
16	rug	15	cooker
17	toaster	18	wardrobe
20	fridge	19	lamp
		21	mirror

Writing

6 *Mögliche Lösung*

I think that in the next 10 years I'll get my own flat, but it's unlikely that I'll leave the town where I live now. I believe that I'll find a job I like. It's possible that I'll change jobs once or twice. I doubt that I'll get married, but I'm sure that I'll find a partner. Maybe my partner will be someone I know now. I doubt that I'll earn a lot of money in my job. I don't know whether I'll visit Australia or New Zealand in the next 10 years. It will be great if I can learn to do something new, for example surfing. For sure I'll meet a lot of new friends.
(117 words)

Video lounge

7   **1**
A–b, B–d C–c, D–a

2
Mögliche Lösung
In this video, Maya, Josh and Greg go to a movie studio in LA. Their guide Carmen tells them that they will meet a movie star there. At the studio, Maya goes to casting and Greg meets his favourite star, Bob Quickpayne. At the end, the three friends are all in one of Mr Quickpayne's movies. I like the video because the scene with Greg and Mr Quickpayne is funny. However, the scene with Maya in casting is boring and I don't like it so much. I would recommend this video because it is a good way to practise your English.
(100 words)

Job pages

Asking for and giving directions

1
1. on the corner of
2. on the left
3. next to
4. on the right
5. opposite

2
1. cross over, opposite
2. take the third turning on the right
3. take the second left, next to
4. past, turn right
5. take the first left

3
next to – *(direkt) neben*
on the corner of – *an der Ecke von*
on the right – *auf der rechten Seite*
on the left – *auf der linken Seite*
opposite – *gegenüber*
cross over – *überqueren*
go past – *vorbeigehen*
take the first left – *nehmen Sie die erste (Straße) links*
take the first right – *nehmen Sie die erste (Straße) rechts*
take the second left – *nehmen Sie die zweite (Straße) links*
take the third turning on the right – *nehmen Sie die dritte Querstraße / Abzweigung rechts*
turn right – *biegen Sie rechts ab*

4 *Mögliche Lösung*
(Building E is a bank, Building D is the post office.)
ME: Excuse me. Is there a bank near here?
MAN: Sure. Go straight up here and take the second left. That's Green Street. The bank is on the right, next to the post office. You can't miss it.
ME: Thanks very much.
MAN: You're welcome.

Getting through on the phone

1

3	How can I help you?	Was kann ich für Sie tun?
4	Could I speak to (name), please?	Ich hätte gern mit (Name) gesprochen.
5	Who is calling please?	Wer ist bitte am Apparat?
6	It's / This is (name) from (country / company).	Hier spricht (Name) (Land / Firma)
7	One moment, please.	Einen Moment, bitte.
8	I'm putting you through now	Ich stelle Sie jetzt durch.
9	I'm sorry	Es tut mir leid
10	(name) is on the phone (at the moment)	(Name) telefoniert gerade
11	(name) isn't in the office (at the moment)	(Name) ist (momentan) nicht im Büro
12	Will you hold?	Möchten Sie warten?
13	Will you call back?	Wollen Sie zurückrufen?
14	Can (name) call you (back)?	Kann (Name) Sie zurückrufen?
15	Sure / Certainly	Sicher
16	I'll hold	Ich warte
17	I'll call back later	Ich rufe später wieder an / zurück
18	Can I take your name, please?	Kann ich bitte Ihren Namen haben / notieren?
19	Can you spell your name for me, please?	Können Sie Ihren Namen bitte buchstabieren?
20	I'll tell (name) that you called	Ich sage (Name) (Bescheid), dass Sie angerufen haben
21	Thanks very much	Vielen Dank
22	Goodbye / Bye (now)	Auf Wiederhören / Tschüss

Can I take a message?

1
1. got, reply
   got, will reply
2. You met, like our products;
   met the new clients, like, products very much
3. go to Berlin, afraid, you can't make the meeting, the 29th, will phone tomorrow to arrange a new time;
   to go to Berlin next week, she's afraid, can't make, on the 29th. She'll phone tomorrow to arrange a new time.
4. are going on holiday from Monday next week and will be away for two weeks. You'll send your monthly report to Mr Cherry on Friday before you leave. If he needs to speak to you urgently, he can use your mobile. The number is 07788 92 34 75 0.
   is going on holiday from Monday next week and will be away for two weeks. He'll send his monthly report to you on Friday before he leaves. If you need to speak to him urgently, you can use his mobile. The number is 07788 92 34 75 0.

2 *Mögliche Lösung*

PA: Christian Wagner.

WOMAN: Good morning, Christian. It's Jenny Lewis here from the London office. Can I speak to Dieter, please?

PA: I'm sorry, Ms Lewis, but he isn't here at the moment. Can I take a message?

WOMAN: Yes, thanks. Can you tell him that I got his email and that I'll send all the information about the next London trade fair to him next week?

PA: I'll just repeat that. You got Mr Schreiner's email and you'll send all the information about the next London trade fair to him next week.

WOMAN: That's right. Thanks, Christian.

PA: You're welcome, Ms Lewis. I'll give Mr Schreiner your message as soon as he's back.

WOMAN: Great. Bye now.

PA: Goodbye.

Telephone message
Date: 4 March
From: Jenny Lewis, London office
Ms Lewis got your email and she will send all the information about the next London trade fair to you next week.

Emails at work

A An: (j.rogers@fairfield...org)
Betreff: Fairfield Festival dates

Dear Jeff

Could you please send me the dates of the
festival this year?
Thanks in advance!

Best wishes

B (Betreff: Fairfield Festival. Jeff schreibt, dass)
das Festival von Freitag, dem 26. Juli bis zum
Sonntag, dem 28. Juli läuft. Er hofft, dass du
kommen willst. Bitte gib ihm Bescheid, wenn du
weitere Informationen bzw. Buchungsformulare
brauchst.

C An: j.rogers@fairfield...org
Betreff: Fairfield Festival

Hi Jeff

Thanks for the dates of the festival. Yes, we want
to come! Could you please send us a booking
form and a list of the other artists who want to
come to the festival this year?

Kind regards

D An: j.kennedy@bristoltourism.co...uk
Betreff: Hotels in Bristol

Dear Ms Kennedy

The German band Metro Dynamite plans to
play in a club in Bristol later this year. Could you
please send us a list of hotels in Bristol which are
not too expensive?

Thanks in advance

Best wishes

Jenny Kennedy hat uns als PDF-Datei eine Liste
von Hotels in Bristol zwischen £50 und £100 pro
Nacht geschickt. Wir sollen uns bei ihr melden,
wenn wir weitere Hilfe brauchen. Sie lässt dich
grüßen, Christian.

Kickoff Foundation Workbook

Dieses Lösungsheft ist
Bestandteil von:

ISBN 978-3-12-**808303**-2

9 783128 083032

Grammar

1 The five people below work for a firm in Danbury called Danbury Windows.
Write two sentences about each person like the example. Be careful with *for* and *since*!

Laura
apprentice carpenter **(1 year)**

Dan
office worker **(2010)**

Michael
warehouse worker **(2008)**

Carolyn
manager **(4 years)**

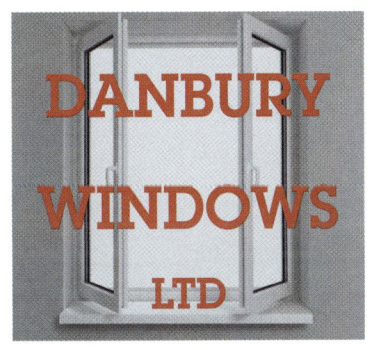

Mrs Ellis
secretary **(a long time!)**

1 Laura _is an apprentice carpenter._
She has worked for the company for one year.

2 Dan _____

_____

3 Michael _____

_____

4 Carolyn _____

_____

5 Mrs Ellis _____

_____ !

_____
→ * for ages: *seit einer Ewigkeit (Umgangssprache)*

Zeitpunkt oder Zeitraum?

Zeitpunkt ●
since 2008, (last) July, Tuesday
(last week), yesterday,
10 o'clock (this morning),
I was 5 years old

Zeitraum ➡
for 3 years, 2 months,
8 weeks, a long time, ages*

2 **Make questions with *How long* for two of the people on page 24 and write their answers.**

Example: How long have you been with the firm, Laura?
    – I've been with them for a year.

1 _____

2 _____

3 **Know your irregular verbs! Complete the table with the *past participles* (3rd form) of these irregular verbs, then use verbs from the table to finish the sentences below about the people in question 1 again. All the verbs are in the *present perfect*.**

Verb	Simple past	3rd form	Verb	Simple past	3rd form
to be	was/were	(1) been	to know	knew	(7) _____
to do	did	(2) _____	to make	made	(8) _____
to drink	drank	(3) _____	to sell	sold	(9) _____
to drive	drove	(4) _____	to sing	sang	(10) _____
to go	went	(5) _____	to spend	spent	(11) _____
to have	had	(6) _____	to wear	wore	(12) _____

1 Laura is an apprentice carpenter at Danbury Windows but in her free time she sings in a band. She
   __has sung__ (to sing) in the band for two years.

2 Michael's hobby is selling things on eBay. He _____ (to sell) things online for about six years.

3 Michael always wears his hat in the warehouse. He _____ (to wear) the same hat every day
   for the last three years!

4 Carolyn likes fast cars. She has a sports car. She _____ (to drive) it since last year.

5 Mrs Ellis loves making cakes. She _____ (to make) cakes since she was a teenager.

6 Dan has a girlfriend called Alice. He _____ (to know) her for three years and next year he
   wants to marry her.

4 ***Present perfect* or *simple past*? Here is another person who lives in Danbury. Complete the text about him with the correct forms of the verbs.**

Anil Chandra is one of Danbury's most successful businessmen.
He runs an internet business called A Taste of India. This is the story of
Anil's life. Anil's family **(1)** __has lived__ (to live) in England for over
40 years. His parents **(2)** _____ (to come) to the country
from India in 1980. At first, they **(3)** _____ (to live) in
Manchester in the north of England and Anil **(4)** _____
(to be born) there in 1983. In 1985, however, the three of them
(5) _____ (to move) to Danbury and so Anil **(6)** _____ (to live) there since he was very
young. As a boy, Anil **(7)** _____ (to grow up) and **(8)** _____ (to go) to school in the
town. Anil's father and mother **(9)** _____ (to have) a shop and in the evenings and at the

weekends, Anil **(10)** _____ (to work) in the shop. When Anil **(11)** _____ (to leave)

school in 2003, he **(12)** _____ (to go) to college where he **(13)** _____ (to study)

business and after that he **(14)** _____ (to work) in his parents' shop again. But Anil soon

(15) _____ (to see) that the world of his parents and his world **(16)** _____ (to be) very

different. There **(17)** _____ (to be) big supermarkets where people **(18)** _____ (can)

buy goods very cheaply. And at the same time, more and more English people **(19)** _____(to

love) Indian food and they **(20)** _____ (to want) to cook it at home. So about four years ago, Anil

(21) _____ (to have) the idea of selling Indian spices* on the internet. That year, the family

(22) _____ (to sell) the shop and Anil **(23)** _____ (to start) his business, A Taste of

India. Anil **(24)** _____ (to run**) the business now for three years. Since he began, the business

(25) _____ (to grow) quickly. In fact, since last year, Anil **(26)** _____ (to employ) five

people to help him. One other thing in Anil's life is also good: two years ago, he **(27)** _____

(to marry) his girlfriend Priya, and since last month they **(28)** _____ (to have) a son. The son has

his father's name, Azim.

Vocabulary

5 **Read the tips box and fill in the missing words in the table – use your dictionary if necessary.**
Then use words from the table to finish the sentences below.

word	opposite
happy	(1) _unhappy_____
successful	(2) _____
regular	(3) _____
to agree	(4) _____
possible	(5) _____
friendly	(6) _____
to like	(7) _____
advantage	(8) _____
perfect	(9) _____
comfortable	(10) _____
employed	(11) _____
usual	(12) _____

╳ **Neue Wörter bilden mit _un-_ usw.**

Oft können wir ein neues Wort bilden, welches die gegenteilige Bedeutung eines anderen Wortes hat, wenn wir am Wortanfang _un-_ anfügen. Z.B.:
happy   **un**happy
Bei manchen Wörtern müssen wir allerdings andere Buchstaben hinzufügen. Die wichtigsten Vorsilben sind: _ir-, im-, dis-_.

1 Jamie Oliver was _unsuccessful_____ at school but very successful later in his life.

2 _To work_ is a regular verb but _to go_ is an _____ verb.

3 There are some things in life that are just not possible: they are _____.

4 He doesn't have a job at the moment: he is _____.

5 Sorry, I _____ with you: I think you're wrong.

6 Should we do this? There are advantages and _____.

_____
→* spices: _Gewürze_   →** to run (a business): _(ein Geschäft) führen, leiten_

6 **Do the crossword. All the words were in the unit.**

Down
1 Lieblings-
2 berühmt
3 Erfolgsgeschichte (2 words)
6 another word for 'company'
7 another word for 'journalist'
9 Angestellte(r)
11 freundlich
12 husband and …
13 plural of 'child'
17 örtlich, Orts- e.g. … newspaper

Across
4 arbeitslos
5 the opposite of 'successful'
8 person who plays music at a party, in a club etc. (2 words)
10 to … money: Geld verdienen
14 unterschiedlich: they all have … jobs
15 legasthenisch
16 Klempner/Klempnerin
18 Polen
19 another word for 'perhaps'
20 to … sb: jmdn heiraten

7 **How many words can you make with the letters in the grid?**

A	C	D	E
E	F	G	H
I	L	M	N
O	R	S	S
T	U	V	Y

an, and, another, ago

Writing

8 You often correspond with some American students on the website CollegeNet. Today, you want to write about the town (or village) where you live. Write a text of around 100 words. Describe your town and say why you like (or don't like) living there. Begin with the words below. There are some phrases to help you.

a town, a village, a big city
*to have (number) inhabitants**
old/new/modern/partly old and partly new
an industrial town
a river called the ... flows through the town
the oldest/buildings are
*park/shop/café/restaurant/cinema/church/ cathedral/town hall***/stadium/pub/ square****/hotel/theatre/ museum/narrow street/wide street/tree/garden/lake*
my favourite place in town is
*if you want to travel around town there are buses/trams/suburban trains****/ underground trains*
attractive/pretty/exciting/dynamic/historic/ fun/friendly/dirty/noisy/unattractive/ crowded/boring/too big/ too small

Today I want to write to you about the place where I live. It's called _____

and I have lived here since_____

_____

_____

_____

_____

_____

_____

Video lounge

9 Watch the video and write in the missing words and phrases.

Jasmine Here she is! Diane, I'd like to introduce John Carter and Paul Rogers from Australian Power Utilities.

Diane **(1)** _____ !

John **(2)** _____ , Ms Kennedy. I'm John Carter.

Diane Please, call me Diane!

John Fine, Diane. And I'm John. **(3)** _____ Paul Rogers.

Paul Pleased to meet you, Diane.

Diane Pleased to meet you too, Paul. And I see you've met my assistant Jasmine already.

(4) _____ . I'm afraid my last **(5)** _____ went on a while.

John Oh, **(6)** _____ . Jasmine took care of us.

Diane Good. So, please have a seat.

Paul Thanks.

→ * inhabitants: *Einwohner*   → ** town hall: *Rathaus*   → *** square: *Platz*   → **** suburban train: *S-Bahn*

Unit 7 Looking ahead

Grammar

1 *Going to* for plans. It is the end of year at a college and the students below are planning a party. The guy on the right is George. He's talking about their plans. Read what he says and answer the questions below in full sentences.

Last year we organised the end-of-year party outside and it rained. So this year, we're going to have it inside in the college sports hall. Last year we had a disco. It was OK, but this year we're going to have a live band. Susie (the girl standing behind me) knows some guys in a band and she's going to contact them. We've got a plan for something totally new this year, too. At midnight, we're going to show* a movie.

1 Where did the students organise the end-of-year party last year?

They organised it outside.

2 Where are George and his friends going to organise the party this year?

They _____

3 What music did they have last year?

_____

4 What music are George und his friends going to have this year?

_____

5 What is Susie going to do?

_____

6 They plan something totally new this year. What are they going to do?

_____

2 *Going to* for plans. Imagine that you are planning a party, too, for your class at college. Use the ideas in exercise 1 to write four things you are going to do for your party. Where are you going to have it? Are you going to have music? What kind of food are you going to have? Do you have an idea for something 'different' (like a movie)?

We are going to have the party _____

_____

_____

_____

_____

→ * to show: *vorführen*

3 *Will future*. **George (from page 34) is at a fair* in town. He's with a fortune teller. Read what she says to George and find the three sentences below which are wrong. Correct the false sentences.**

You'll be married but your wife won't be from England. You'll live with her in another country. You'll have lots of children – ah, they'll all be girls. You won't be rich but you won't be poor. You'll have three jobs in your life. You'll like the first job, but you'll hate the second. You won't have that job very long. The best job will be the third. Something bad will happen when you're 30 and your life will be hard for two or three years. But everything will be OK after that your life will be long and happy

A George won't be rich or poor.
B He'll die when he's 30.
C His wife won't be English.
D George's best job will be his second job.

E George will live in another country.
F All George's children will be boys.
G His life will be long and happy.
H George will like his first job.

1 Sentence _B___ : George won't _die_ _____

   Something _____

2 Sentence _____

   _____

3 Sentence _____

   _____

Vocabulary

4 **Verbs with *to look*. Read the box on the right, then finish the sentences with the correct prepositions.**

1 The students in this unit are looking _____ – they're thinking about their life in the future.

2 Nurses look _____ patients in hospital.

3 Are you looking _____ the holidays? – Yes, very much!

4 I've lost my phone. I've looked _____ it everywhere but can't find it.

5 You can use an online dictionary to look _____ words you don't understand.

6 Look _____! That car is coming down the street very fast!

7 Look _____ the sunset**. Isn't it beautiful?

✛ **Verben + Präpositionen**

Im Englischen erhält man neue Verben, wenn man unterschiedliche Präpositionen an ein Verb wie z.B. *to look* anhängt:

- *to look ahead*: vorausschauen, nach vorne schauen
- *to look at*: anschauen, betrachten
- *to look after*: sich kümmern um, aufpassen auf
- *to look up*: nachschauen, nachschlagen
- *to look forward to*: sich freuen auf, freudig erwarten
- *to look for*: suchen
- *to look out*: aufpassen

→ * fair: *Jahrmarkt, Volksfest*   → ** sunset: *Sonnenuntergang*

5 **Try this crossword. All the words are things you can find in a house or flat (*AE* apartment).**

Down

1 part of a flat, house etc. This is the sleeping … (*Bereich*)
3 (in the bathroom) you wash your hands in this
4 a table where you eat (2 words)
5 the place / door where you come in
6 you know the time when you look at this
11 I'm going to … my flat blue. (*streichen*)
13 (in the kitchen) an electric … . You heat water in this. (*Wasserkessel*)
16 you put this on the floor (*Vorleger*)
17 you make toast with this
20 (in the kitchen) this keeps food, milk etc. cool

Across

2 (in the bathroom) you stand in this and water comes down on your head to make you clean
7 a plant which grows indoors, usually in a pot
8 There is a clock on this … (*Wand*)
9 you can put notes, pictures, calendars – lots of things on this (*Pinnwand*)
10 Do we have any spaghetti in the …? (*Schrank*)
12 (in the kitchen) you wash dishes in this (*Spülbecken*)
14 (in the kitchen) if you put food in this, it becomes hot very quickly
15 you cook food on this. Some are electric, some are gas.
18 (in a bedroom) you hang your clothes in it
19 Switch on that … - it's dark.
21 you can see yourself when you look in a …

Writing

6 **Looking ahead. First answer the questions in the questionnaire, then use your answers to write a text about yourself. There are some useful phrases to help you. Write about 100 words. Write on a separate piece of paper.**

WHAT WILL HAPPEN IN YOUR LIFE IN THE NEXT 10 YEARS?

1 I'll get my own flat or house.
  ○ Yes   ○ No   ○ Don't know

2 I'll leave the town where I live now to live somewhere else.
  ○ Yes   ○ No   ○ Don't know

3 I'll find a job I like.
  ○ Yes   ○ No   ○ Don't know

4 I'll change jobs / where I work at least once.
  ○ Yes   ○ No   ○ Don't know

5 I'll get married or find a partner.
  ○ Yes   ○ No   ○ Don't know

6 My partner will be someone I know now.
  ○ Yes   ○ No   ○ Don't know

7 I'll have a child.
  ○ Yes   ○ No   ○ Don't know

8 I'll earn a lot of money / be rich
  ○ Yes   ○ No   ○ Don't know

9 I'll visit the USA, Britain, Australia or New Zealand.
  ○ Yes   ○ No   ○ Don't know

10 I'll see my favourite band or singer in concert / meet a famous person.
  ○ Yes   ○ No   ○ Don't know

11 I'll learn to do something new (how to play a new sport, for example).
  ○ Yes   ○ No   ○ Don't know

12 I'll meet some new friends.
  ○ Yes   ○ No   ○ Don't know

USEFUL PHRASES

I think I'm sure / certain I believe*	that	in the next 10 years	I'll …
I don't think I doubt I think it's unlikely**	that	in the next 10 years	I'll …
I (honestly***) don't know	if / whether	I'll …	in the next 10 years
I don't know	but	I (really) hope that	I'll …
It will be	great	if I can …	in the next 10 years
It's possible / probable****	that	I'll …	but I don't know (for sure*****)
Maybe	I'll …	but	maybe I won't
I think	that	I'll …	because …
I …	now	so I think I'll …	in the future

→ * to believe: *glauben* → ** unlikely: *unwahrscheinlich* → *** honestly: *ehrlich(erweise)*
→ **** probable: *wahrscheinlich* → ***** for sure: *ganz bestimmt*

Video lounge

7 **Write a review of the video on a separate piece of paper.**

  1 Watch the video. Put the stills (*Standbilder*) A–D in the right order and find the parts of the script (*Drehbuch*) a–d which go with each still.

  2 Write your review. The box below (on the right) and the useful phrases will help you.

a	**Casting director**	I've got a role for you. And didn't you say you have two friends here with you?
	Maya	Yeah.
b	**Greg**	Hi! Bob, I mean Quickpayne, Mr Quickpayne, hi. I've waited my whole life to meet you personally. This is so exciting. I mean, me and you …
		Quickpayne shakes Greg's hand.
c	**Carmen**	Listen: I have a great surprise for you. On your last day in the United States, I've arranged for you to meet a movie star!
d	**Josh**	I can't believe I'm doing this. Appearing in a film that's probably the worst B-movie ever made.

USEFUL PHRASES

Summarising the plot
In this video, the main characters (names) …
Their guide Carmen tells them …
Maya goes to … / Greg …
At the end, they …
Giving your opinion
I like / don't like the video because …
I think that the part where (Greg / Maya …) is funny / silly / interesting / boring / …
Recommending the movie
I would / wouldn't recommend this video to other people.

Filminhalte wiedergeben
Wenn man die Inhalte eines Films (Videoclips oder Buchs) zusammenfasst, verwendet man das *simple present.*
*In this movie / video the characters **visit** a studio.*
*Greg **meets** his favourite star.*

Anhang
Job pages
Vocabulary by themes

Asking for and giving directions

1 **Giving directions. Where are the buildings? Finish the sentences with the correct words and phrases. Remember: you are walking from the bottom of the map towards the top.**

> next to – on the corner of –
> on the left – on the right – opposite

1   Building A is _____

    West Street and North Street.

2   Go up North Street. Building B is _____

    _____. You can't miss it!

3   Building B is _____ Building C.

4   Go straight up North Street. Building D is _____

    You can't miss it!

5   Building D is _____ Building B.

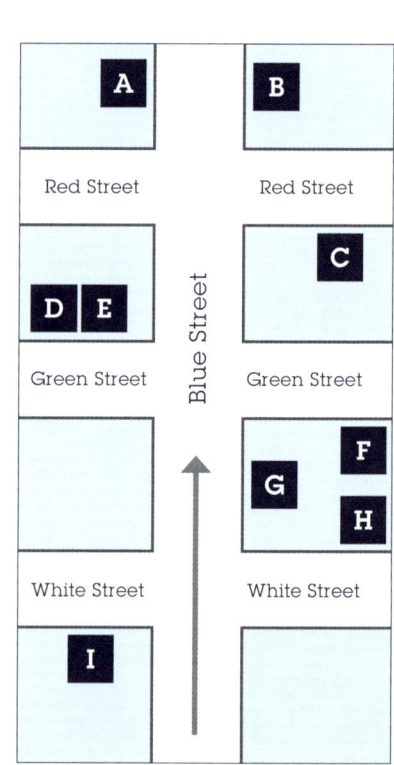

2 **Giving directions. Now complete the directions below and on the next page with the correct words and phrases. You are walking from the bottom towards the top of the map again.**

> cross over – next to – opposite – past –
> take the first left – take the first right –
> take the second left
> take the third turning on the right
> turn right

1   Building A? Yes, go straight up here,

    _____ White Street,

    Green Street and Red Street and it's on your left. It's

    _____ Building B.

2   Building C? Mmm OK. Go up Blue Street and

    _____. It's on the right.

    You can't miss it!

3   Building D? Sure. Go straight up here and _____. It's on the

right, _____ Building E.

4   Building F? OK, go up here, go _____ Building G and

_____. That's Green Street. Building F is on your right. It's not far.

5   Building H? Right, go along here and _____. You can't miss it!

6   Building I? That's easy. Go up here and _____. It's up there about a

hundred meters on yout left.

3 **Write in German words and phrases for the expressions you used in tasks 1 and 2.**

next to	(direkt) neben	take the first left	
on the corner of		take the first right	
on the right		take the second left	
on the left		take the third turning on the right	
opposite			
cross over		turn right	
go past			

4 **Asking for and giving directions. You are visiting the English town of which you can see a map in task 2.**

1   First, think of places in the town which could be Buildings A to I. For example, Building A is the post office, Building B a café.
2   You are at the bottom of the map in Blue Street.
3   Choose a place on the map which you want to go to. Write a conversation below with a passer-by – you ask for directions and the English person gives them to you. Use the phrases from tasks 1 to 3 above and from your book on page 107.
4   Write more conversations on a separate piece of paper until you are sure of all the phrases and can use them easily.

ME: Excuse me. _____

_____

_____

_____

_____

_____

_____

_____

_____

_____

_____

_____

Getting through on the phone

1 Here is a list of useful phrases that you can use when you are on the phone. Write in the German translations.

English	Deutsch
1 Good morning	*Guten Morgen*
2 (name) speaking	*Sie sprechen mit (Namen)*
3 How can I help you?	
4 Could I speak to (name), please?	
5 Who is calling please?	
6 It's/This is (name) from (country/company)	
7 One moment, please	
8 I'm putting you through now	
9 I'm sorry	
10 (name) is on the phone (at the moment)	
11 (name) isn't in the office (at the moment)	
12 Will you hold?	
13 Will you call back?	
14 Can (name) call you (back)?	
15 Sure/Certainly	
16 I'll hold	
17 I'll call back later	
18 Can I take your name, please?	
19 Can you spell your name for me, please?	
20 I'll tell (name) that you called	
21 Thanks very much	
22 Goodbye/Bye (now)	

2 You work for a German marketing company called GEM Marktforschung where you are the assistant to Herr Schmitz. You get the phone call below from someone in England. Complete the dialogue with suitable phrases.

You   GEM Marktforschung. **(1)** _____ *(Sie sprechen mit …).* **(2)** _____

(Was kann ich für Sie tun?)

Caller   Good morning. This is Carol Evans from Alpha Software in England. Can I speak to Mr Schmitz, please?

You   **(3)** _____ *(Einen Moment, bitte. Ich verbinde Sie.)*

Caller   Thanks.

3 **A few minutes later, you get another call. This time, your boss Mr Schmitz is on the phone. Complete the dialogue with suitable phrases.**

You GEM Marktforschung. **(1)** _____ *(Sie sprechen mit …).* **(2)** _____

   (Was kann ich für Sie tun?)

Caller Oh, hi. This is Judith Snyder from the LPT&T Advertising Agency in New York. Can I speak to Mr

   Schmitz, please?

You **(3)** _____ *(Es tut mir leid. Herr Schmitz telefoniert gerade.)* **(4)** _____

   (Möchten Sie warten?)

Caller Sure, no problem. …

You Hello, Ms Snyder? Mr Schmitz is free now. **(5)** _____ *(Ich verbinde Sie.)*

Caller Thanks.

4 **It's now afternoon. Mr Schmitz is not in the office this afternoon. Complete the dialogue below with suitable phrases.**

You GEM Marktforschung. **(1)** _____ *(Ihr Name)* speaking. How can I help you?

Caller Good afternoon. Could I speak to Mr Schmitz, please?

You **(2)** _____

   (Es tut mir leid. Herr Schmitz ist heute nachmittag nicht im Haus.)

   (3) _____

   (Kann er Sie morgen früh zurückrufen?)

Caller It's probably easier if I call him tomorrow morning. I may not be at my desk all morning.

YOU That's fine. **(4)** _____ *(Geben Sie mir bitte Ihren Namen?)*

Caller Yes, it's Ken Kobayashi from SENJI Electronics in Dusseldorf.

YOU **(5)** _____

   _____

   (Wie schreibt man bitte Ihren Namen?)

Caller Ken Kobayashi, K-E-N, K-O-B-A-Y-A-S-H-I.

YOU **(6)** _____

   _____

   _____

   (Vielen Dank, Herr Kobayashi. Ich sage

   Herrn Schmitz, dass Sie angerufen haben.)

Caller Great, thanks. Bye now.

YOU **(7)** _____ *(Auf Wiederhören.)*

Can I take a message?

1 Jayne is a PA and her boss is Mr Williams. Mr Williams isn't in the office today and Jayne is taking messages. Look at the three pictures and short texts, then complete more of Jayne's conversations and messages below.

MR WILLIAMS: Can you tell Mr Cherry that I'll be in London next week and that I'd like to meet him?

JAYNE: I'll just repeat that. You'll be in London next week and you would like to meet Mr Cherry.

JAYNE WRITES THE MESSAGE: Mr Williams will be in London next week and he would like to meet you.

1 **MS PARKER**:
Can you tell Mr Cherry that I got his email and that I'll reply as soon as I can?

JAYNE:

I'll just repeat that. You _____

Mr Cherry's email and you will _____

as soon as you can.

JAYNE WRITES THE MESSAGE:

Ms Parker _____ your email

and she _____ as soon as she can.

2 **MR WARD:**
Can you tell Mr Cherry that I met the new clients last week and they like our products and prices very much?

JAYNE:

I'll just repeat that. _____

_____ the new clients last

week and they _____

_____ very much.

JAYNE WRITES THE MESSAGE:

Mr Ward _____ last week and they _____ our

_____

3 **MS WEST:**
Can you tell Mr Cherry that I have to go to Berlin next week so I'm afraid I can't make our meeting on the 29th. I'll phone tomorrow to arrange a new time.

Nachrichten entgegennehmen

Wenn man am Telefon eine Nachricht entgegennimmt, um sie an eine dritte Person weiterzugeben, sind drei verschiedene sprachliche Versionen zu berücksichtigen:

1 Die Aussage des Sprechers: sie enthält *I*, *my*, *our* usw.
   I will be in London next week.
2 Die Rückfrage, ob man die zu übermittelnde Nachricht richtig verstanden hat: hier benutzt man *you*, *your* usw.
   You will be in London next week.
3 Die Nachricht selbst, die an eine dritte Person übermittelt wird: sie enthält den Namen des Anrufers und *(s)he*, *her/his* usw.
   Ms Lewis/She will be in London next week.

JAYNE:

I'll just repeat that. You have to _____ next week

and you are _____ that _____ with Mr Cherry

on _____ . You _____

_____ .

JAYNE WRITES THE MESSAGE:

Ms West has _____ so _____ that

she _____ your meeting _____

_____

4   **MR DAVIS:**
I'm going on holiday from Monday next week and will be away for two weeks. I'll send my monthly report to Mr Cherry on Friday before I leave. If he needs to speak to me urgently, he can use my mobile. The number is 07788 92 34 75 0.

JAYNE:

I'll just repeat that. You _____

_____

_____

_____

JAYNE WRITES THE MESSAGE:

Mr Davis _____

_____

_____

_____

2   **Now you. Think of a telephone conversation between a PA and a caller. Think of the the date, names of firms, the PA's boss's name and the details of the conversation yourself. Write the conversation below, then write a telephone message for the call. Begin with the PA as in your book on pages 110–111.**

_____

_____

_____

_____

_____

TELEPHONE MESSAGE

Date: _____

From: _____

_____

_____

_____

Emails at work

Organising concerts for musicians is a lot of work and bands need people who do this for them. You work for the German band Metro Dynamite. Later this year, the band plans to go on a tour of the UK. You are going to organise some aspects of their tour.

A Here is a note from Christian Treiber, the band's lead singer. Read the note and complete the email below.

> Bitte schicke eine E-Mail an einen Mann, der Jeff Rogers heißt (E-Mail-Adresse: j.rogers@fairfield...org). Jeff (nenne ihn bei seinem Vornamen) organisiert jedes Jahr das Fairfield Music Festival. Verwende die Betreffzeile: ‚Fairfield Festival-Daten' und frage ihn nach den Daten für das Festival in diesem Jahr. Schreibe ihm ‚Danke im Voraus!'.

An: _j.rogers@fairfield...org_ _____

Betreff: _____

_____

_____

_____

_____

B You get this reply from Jeff. Write a note for Christian in German.

Von: j.rogers@fairfield...org
Subject: Fairfield Festival

Hi!
Thanks for your email about the festival this year. The dates are Friday 26 – Sunday 28 July. Hope that you want to come! Just tell me if you want more information, booking forms* etc.
All the best
Jeff

Betreff: Fairfield Festival. Jeff
schreibt, dass _____

_____

_____

_____

_____

_____

→ * booking form: *Buchungsformular*

C Christian asks you to write a second email to Jeff at the Fairfield Festival. Here are his notes. Write the email.

> Beantworte Jeffs E-Mail. Bedanke dich für die Daten und sage ihm, dass wir zum Festival kommen möchten. Könnte er uns bitte ein Buchungsformular schicken? Ach ja, und hat er eine Liste der anderen Künstler, die dieses Jahr zum Festival kommen wollen?

An: _____

Betreff: _____

_____

_____

_____

_____

_____

D Now Christian asks you to send another email. Look at his notes and write the email on a separate sheet of paper.

> Ich habe gerade zugesagt, dass wir auf unserer Tour in einem Club im Zentrum von Bristol auftreten. Könntest du bitte eine E-Mail zum dortigen Tourismusverband schicken? Bitte sie, uns eine Liste mit Hotels in Bristol, die nicht zu teuer sind, zuzuschicken. Bedanke dich im Voraus. Ich habe letztes Jahr einer Frau dort geschrieben. Ihre E-Mail-Adresse ist: j.kennedy@ bristoltourism. co…uk.

E You get this reply. Write a note for Christian in German.

Von: j.kennedy@bristoltourism.co…uk
Subject: hotels in Bristol

Dear … (your name)
Many thanks for your email about hotels in Bristol. Attached as a PDF is a list of hotels in the city that are between £50 and £100 per night. Please let me know if you would like any further help. And say 'hello' to Christian from me!
Kind regards
Jenny Kennedy

Jenny Kennedy hat _____

_____

_____

_____

_____

_____

_____

Vocabulary by themes

On these pages, the most important vocabulary you have learned is arranged by themes. For each theme:

1 write in the German translations of the word or phrase;
2 choose ten words or phrases and write an example sentence for each on a separate piece of paper or in your vocabulary notebook.

NOTE: AE = American English; BE = British English.

1 Occupations (Berufe)

Tips and tricks
- Berufe stehen im Englischen immer mit dem Artikel *a/an*:
  *He is **a** mechanic.*
  *I want to become **an** actor.*
  ~~He is mechanic.~~
  ~~I want to become actor.~~
- Berufsbezeichnungen enden häufig auf *-ian*, *-er* oder *-or*.

actor

admin(istrative) assistant

apprentice

building/construction worker

businessman/
    businesswoman/
    businessperson

career

to choose a career

computer/IT technician

cook/chef

dentist

dental assistant

(film) director

doctor

doctor's receptionist

driver (e.g. bus/lorry driver)

electrician

employee

factory worker

fitness trainer

footballer

full-time job

gardener

hairdresser

hostel warden

hotel worker/receptionist

journalist/reporter

mechanic

musician

nurse

nursery assistant

office worker

painter (and decorator)

part-time job

personal assistant (PA)

pharmacist

photographer

plumber

police officer

postman/postwoman

receptionist

shop assistant

singer

technician

volunteer

waiter/waitress

2 Workplaces (Arbeitsplätze)

Tips and tricks

Suche zu den Arbeitsplätzen
die passenden Berufe in
Abschnitt 1 und schreibe
Beispielsätze:

A chef works in a kitchen.
A factory worker ...

airport

beauty salon

building/construction site

company/firm

department (of a company)

doctor's/dental practice

factory

fitness club/gym

garden/park

hairdressing salon

head office

hospital

(youth) hostel

hotel

kitchen

marketing company

nursery

office

pharmacy

post office

restaurant

shop (AE store|)

swimming pool/sports centre

workshop

Other useful expressions:

indoors

outdoors

rules (in the workplace)

hard hat

sign

3 Towns and cities (Städte und Großstädte)

Tips and tricks

- Menschen leben und arbeiten in Städten, deshalb sind einige der Orte in diesem Abschnitt auch in Abschnitt 2 zu finden.
- Die häufigste Präposition bei Ortsangaben ist *at*: *at* the railway station, *at* the museum. Aber: *in* the park/the town centre/I live *in* … (Name der Stadt).
- Bei Straßennamen steht die Präposition *in*: The restaurant is *in* Canal Street. ~~The restaurant is on (the) Canal Street.~~

bank

bus station

café

capital (city)

car park

cinema; (AE) movie theater

college

high street; (AE) main street

hotel

museum

park

pharmacy

population

(BE) pub

railway station

school

shopping precinct; (AE) mall

street

swimming pool/sport centre

town/city centre;
  (AE downtown)

traffic lights

Useful phrases:

Excuse me. How do I get to
  ...?

I'm looking for ...

Can you tell me the way to
  ...?

Is there a ... near here?

4 Free time activities (Freizeitaktivitäten)

✝Tips and tricks

* Wenn es um Freizeitaktivitäten geht, braucht man die Ausdrücke **I like ...** und **I'm not keen on** ... und es steht häufig die **-ing**-Form der Verben:
  I like **playing** the piano.
  I'm not keen on **shopping**.
* Im Englischen bist du *good at sth*:
  I'm good **at** sport.
  ~~I'm good in sport.~~

athletics

baking cakes

cooking/cookery

cycling

doing karate/sports/yoga/

going online

going to the cinema/gym

hanging out with friends

inline skating

keeping fit

listening to music

making jewellery

playing football/hockey/
basketball/video games

playing the piano/the guitar

reading

shopping

skateboarding

snowboarding

social networking

swimming

texting friends

travelling

vegging

watching TV

working part time

Useful phrases:

to like/love doing sth

to be/not to be keen on
doing sth

to be good at sth

5 Homes (Wohnsitze)

Tips and tricks

- Beachte den Unterschied zwischen *home* und *at home*:
  I am **at home** at the moment.
  Ich bin momentan **zu Hause**.
  *She went **home** after her lessons.*
  Sie ging nach dem Unterricht **nach Hause**.
  ~~She went at home.~~
- In englischen und amerikanischen Adressen steht die Hausnummer vor dem Straßennamen:
  14 Park Street
  ~~Park Street 14~~

address

bathroom

bedroom

bedside cabinet

clock

coffee table

cooker

cupboard

desk

dining room

electric kettle

entrance

flat, (AE apartment)

floor

fridge

houseplant

kettle

lamp

microwave

mirror

patio

pinboard

rug

shower

sink

sofa

to paint sth

toaster

wall

wardrobe

washbasin

window

6 Media and the internet (Medien und Internet)

Tips and tricks

Beachte, dass bei Wörtern wie Radio, Fernsehen und Internet die Präposition *on* steht:
*I watched a good programme **on** (the) TV yesterday evening.*
*You can find lots of information **on** the internet.*

blog/to blog/blogger

email

email address

to write/send an email

to email sb

to reply to answer an email

internet

internet search engine

mass/social media

message

to post a message

mobile (phone); (AE) cell
  (phone)

news (singular!)

newspaper

questionnaire

radio

screen name

social networking site

to join a networking site

television/TV/the telly

to watch TV

TV show/series

to go online

to listen to the radio/music

web page

website

World Wide Web (www. . . .)

7 Telephone phrases (Telefonieren)

Tips and tricks

Beachte!

- Im britischen Englisch *you speak to somebody*:
  *I spoke **to** her yesterday.*
  ~~I spoke with her yesterday.~~
- Im Englischen steht in vielen Ausdrücken *will*, während im Deutschen das Präsens verwendet wird:
  Ich rufe Sie zurück.
  ***I'll call** you back.*

Can (s)he call you (back)?

Can I take a message?

Can I/Could I speak to (name),
  please?

Can you tell her/him that . . .

Good morning/Good
 afternoon

Goodbye/Bye now

Hello/Hi.

How are you?

I'll call you back (later).

I'll give (name) your message
 as soon as (s)he's back.

I'll just repeat that.

I'm afraid (that) . . .

I'm fine, thanks (and you?).

I'm putting you through now

I'm sorry (but) . . .

Thanks (very much).

This is (name) from (place/
 company)

Will you call back?

Will you hold?

You're welcome.

8 EU countries (EU Länder)

Can you find and write in the 10 missing EU countries?

RECEEG   LATYI   GROUBMUXEL   THERNLANDES   PLANDO   MORANIA

~~NEDKRAM~~   PAINS   DEWNES

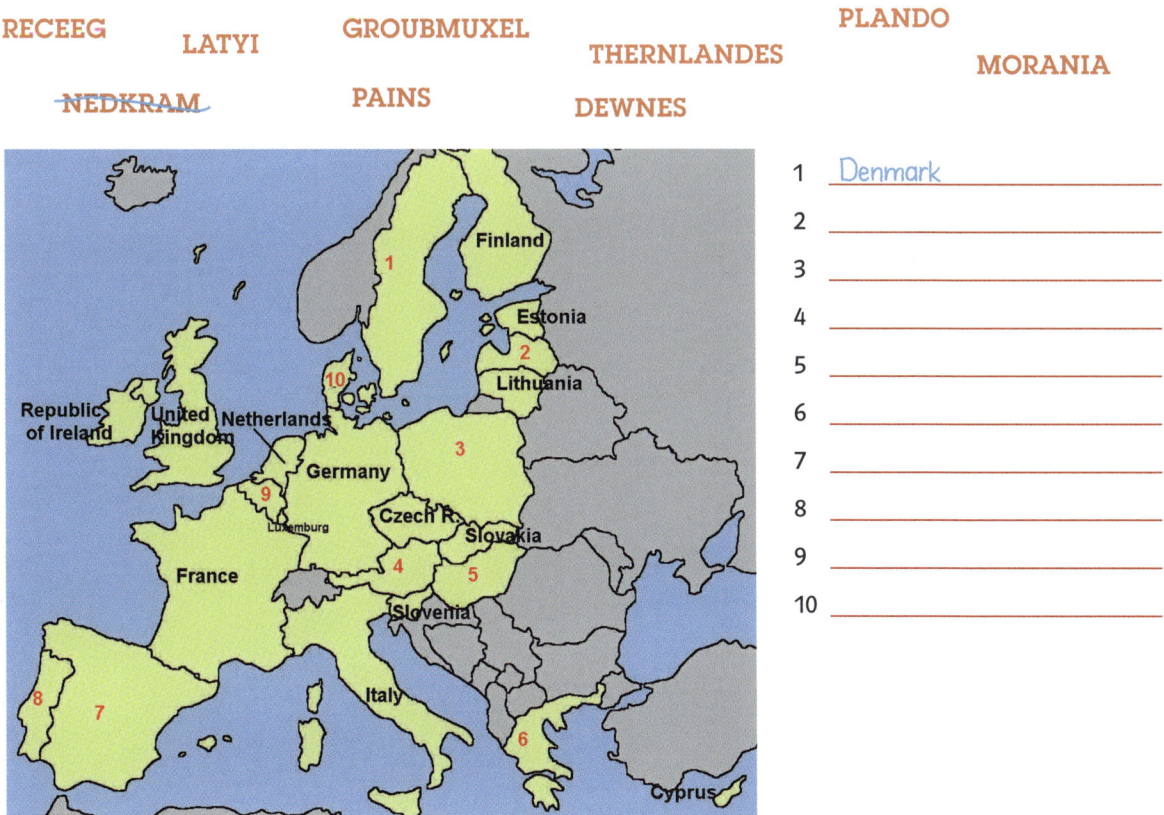

1 Denmark

2 _____

3 _____

4 _____

5 _____

6 _____

7 _____

8 _____

9 _____

10 _____

9 Useful words (Nützliche Wörter)

Tips and tricks

Beachte!
Es ist wichtig, beim Lernen von Adjektiven und Verben gleich die ganze Wendung oder den Satz zu lernen, in dem das Wort häufig gebraucht wird. Lerne z.B. nicht nur das Adjektiv *brilliant*, sondern gleich die Wendung: *That's a brilliant idea!*

brilliant

careful

different

difficult/hard

exciting

expensive

famous

fascinating

favourite

important

necessary

popular

possible/impossible

strange

successful/unsuccessful

to change sth

to describe sth

to explain

to get on (well) with sb

to happen

to imagine

to make a mistake

to marry sb

to mean

to remember sth/to do sth

to solve (a problem)

extremely

immediately

particularly

probably

unfortunately